O LOVELY GLOWWORM

or

Scenes of Great Beauty

Glen Berger

ANDREW
MARVELL

BROADWAY PLAY PUBLISHING INC
56 E 81st St., NY NY 10028-0202
212 772-8334 fax: 212 772-8358
BroadwayPlayPubl.com

O LOVELY GLOWWORM
© Copyright 2006 by Glen Berger

First printing: December 2006
I S B N: 0-88145-290-4

Book design: Marie Donovan
Word processing: Microsoft Word
Typographic controls: Ventura Publisher
Typeface: Palatino
Printed and bound in the U S A

ABOUT THE AUTHOR

Glen Berger launched his playwriting career in earnest as a member of Annex Theater in Seattle. He has spent the last decade in New York.

His UNDERNEATH THE LINTEL played over four hundred performances Off-Broadway and won the 2001 L A Ovation Award and the 2004 Edmonton Sterling Award for Best Play, and was one of *Time Out* New York's Ten Best Plays of 2001.

Other plays include THE WOODEN BREEKS (nominated for Best Writing by the *L A Weekly*, 2001), GREAT MEN OF SCIENCE, NOS. 21 & 22 (1998 Ovation Award and 1998 *L A Weekly* Award for Best Play), and I WILL GO...I WILL GO (published in Applause Book's *2001 Best Short Plays* anthology).

Glen has received a Manhattan Theater Club/Sloan Foundation Fellowship, a Children's Theater of Minneapolis Commission, participated in the 2003 Old Vic/New Voices program, and the 2001 A S K Playwrights Retreat.

He has also written several episodes for the P B S children's series *Arthur* (for which he was nominated for two Emmys), and also its spin-off *Postcards from Buster* (one Emmy nomination), *Time Warp Trio* (N B C), *Peep* (The Learning Channel), and is head writer for *Fetch* (P B S).

He is a member of New Dramatists and lives with his wife and two children.

O LOVELY GLOWWORM was originally produced at Portland Center Stage (Chris Coleman, Artistic Director; Edith Love, Managing Director) opening on 22 March 2005. The cast and creative contributors were:

THE GOAT (also TRUANT OFFICER, TAXIDERMIST, ELDER
  HALLIWELL, OLD SOLDIER, CLERK, & UNICORN)
 .... Ebbe Roe Smith
MARVEAUX .... Troy West
MACMANN .... Tim True
MOTHER/KATHLEEN .... Sharonlee McLean
PHILOMEL .... Christine Calfas
HALLIWELL ....Jim Iorio

Director ....Randy White
Set design .... Lauren Helpern
Lighting design .... Tyler Micoleau
Costume design .... Junghyun Georgia Lee
Sound design .... Jen Raynack
Puppet maker .... Demetri Pavlotos
Fight director ....John Armour
Stage manager .... Mark Tynan
Dramaturg .... Mead Hunter

CHARACTERS

GOAT
MARVEAUX
MACMANN
MOTHER
TRUANT OFFICER*
PHILOMEL
HALLIWELL
TAXIDERMIST*
ELDER HALLIWELL*
OFFSTAGE SOLDIER
KATHLEEN
OLD SOLDIER*
CLERK*
UNICORN*

*played by same actor as GOAT

KATHLEEN and MOTHER should double; as should
HALLIWELL and OFFSTAGE SOLDIER. Consequently,
six actors are required—four men, two women.

The actor supplying the voice of the GOAT should also be
the one manipulating the movements of the GOAT. Except
at the first reveal of the GOAT, the actor/puppeteer should be
seen (to varying degrees) operating the GOAT. A suggested
costume for the actor/puppeteer is a dingy old-fashioned
union suit. When the actor must play one of his other roles,
a jacket or other simple clothing item can be worn. Trousers
are never required.

TIME & PLACE

Shorter Answer:

Time: Now

Place: The GOAT's imagination

Longer Answer:

After being dead for an unknown number of years, the GOAT *has been revived to a sort of consciousness by an ever-increasing pain; but being blind, deaf, and alone, neither he nor we have any idea where he currently is or what year it might be.*

However, as the GOAT *spent nearly all of his more-robust life tethered to a post near a rubbish heap by a cottage outside Dublin between 1910 and 1924, his memories and the inspirations for his "scenes of great beauty" (i.e., his "inner world") should be confined to that place and period.*

Only with the final image of the play do we understand that the GOAT *has* actually *been part of a lovely crèche scene the entire time. The* GOAT *remains unaware of this fact.*

NOTES

Sincerity is crucial (obvious I know, but I feel better
saying it) —stupefying banalities as well as professions
of pain, rapture, and misery should all be delivered
with a solemn intensity and earnestness, tears welling
in the eyes. The songs were inspired by (or directly
lifted from) the songs sung by John McCormack, Henry
Burr, Gene Austin, and other tenors from the first part
of the twentieth century. Other instrumental music,
gleaned from old 78s, is strongly suggested. The set
should rely heavily on scraps of paper and bits of
string, which, in the GOAT's mind's eye, become the
most fantastic of landscapes—shimmering lakes,
cityscapes, battlegrounds, etc. The set may also contain
enlarged swatches of words, images from product
packaging, and photographs, all suggesting contents
of a rubbish heap in Ireland circa 1908-1923.

ACT ONE

(In darkness, strings as they would be heard on a phonograph, circa 1919. Distant, then closer. Faintly heard, singing along, the strained, faltering, earnest voice of an old man.)

VOICE: Troubles and worries may darken the day
Shadows la la the sunshine away
Dreams may la la la
The land and the sea
La la la moonlight..la la...

(Isolated light up slowly to reveal the singer to be a tattered, taxidermically stuffed GOAT, *with expressive brows and a movable jaw.)*

GOAT: La... La La... La...

(The music fades. GOAT *continues singing, then stops. Pause.)*

GOAT: I don't understand any of this. I once was dead, I'm sure of it. Now I'm living. Again! If you can call it living. I can't see a thing. No. Can't hear neither. Smell? No. How about taste? Can I taste? No. Feel though. That I can do. *Feel.* And what is it that I feel? If I had to put a word to it? "Bastarding and bastarding torture" that's what. *(Brightly)* Oh yes, ever-blooming. Like a thousand million slivers of glass running in and out of me. But I can't do it justice. *(Naive and bewildered)* It *hurts*...and it won't stop, and it's getting worse. In fact, I think it's precisely this ever-increasing pain that has revived me again to life. Bah. I'm full of theories. It's facts I'm short of. What the source of this pain is, for instance. That, I don't know. Where I am, that too I don't know. What I am, I don't know. Do I know anything? No. Only that there is pain, and therefore, Life. *(Pause)* And I don't find that very interesting. *But.* There *is* something I find *very* interesting. *(Confiding)* I cannot see or hear the world beyond my eyes and ears, no, but I've constructed, with great effort, an *inner* world, and it's lovely! And I can see it, and I can hear it. I can't taste it, and that's a blow, but I can see it, and I can hear it. And I turn to this inner world again and again for soothing and solace. And here it is—

(Flourish of music. Small pool of light on a man, who looks dead, on the ground. He is wearing a W W I soldier's uniform, his rifle close by his side. We hear, faintly, the sounds of a forest.)

GOAT: Lovely Lovely! Marveaux I call him. I don't know why. The moon, the stars, and he, sleeping. Lovely. *A Scene of Great Beauty.* Through all sorts of weather too. Rainfall...

(We hear a terrible storm, and see water drizzling on MARVEAUX*)*

GOAT: The ground beneath him a sea of mud. It's nothing to him. Snowfall too.

(We see, accompanied by gentle music, snow descending upon him.)

GOAT: Isn't that lovely! And sleet. Feet of it.

(A brief rain of pebbles on him)

GOAT: What solace there is in that—to watch a great man sleeping through adversity. Also leaf fall.

(We hear blustery gusts and a number of leaves fall upon MARVEAUX.*)*

GOAT: And more rain.

(We hear thunder again)

GOAT: And the droppings of birds.

(We hear the caw of crows, and a rain of feathers)

GOAT: And finally...excrement flung by monkeys.

(We see a rather muddy example land on MARVEAUX *from above.)*

GOAT: And...a little more rain.

(We see more water drizzling. Then lights out on MARVEAUX. *Pause)*

GOAT: The end. *(Pause)* Now then. I said I don't know what I am. It's true. But I have *theories*. The most likely theory, of what I am, is..."tramcar conductor." Yes, for I remember the ring of the conductor's bell, the rumble of the wheels on the rails. No doubt I was the man at the throttle. And a lovely life it was—tramcar conducting.... There are worse things to be. For instance, a goat. At least I'm not one of those. Good God. Tethered to a post all of a life! Behind a house, next to a rubbish heap, in driving rain. Horrible. I imagine. To not be a tramcar conductor at all, but only *hear* the approach of the tram in the distance, and the passing of it down the street again. Frightening. For the only bits of beauty for such a creature would be the scraps from the rubbish heap blowing in front of me, him rather, goat, before blowing away again. A photograph in a newspaper, for instance, of a man asleep. I think asleep. The caption— "One of the Hun felled in Flanders Field." *(He cries out as pain increases—)* I..don't..want to be alive. It hurts! *(Desperately)* Back to inner world!

(Lights up on MARVEAUX)

GOAT: Marveaux—how do you manage it?! By being asleep, that's how. What would you do if you were

awake? Should I awaken him? With perhaps...
(Thinks).... a stabbing pain in the head.

(MARVEAUX *wakes up with a short scream, startled and
panicked.*)

MARVEAUX: I'm up! I'm awake! It hurts! I'm up! *(Pause)*
Good. And now we need to get on, or all is lost. *(Panics)*
But why is it so dark? Where am I? Am I dead?!
Where's my hat?! Why must life be such a struggle?!
Ah, here's my hat. *(Brightens)* Yes, I remember now...
a short nap we took, to rest from our flight. But
judging from the sky, I must have dozed longer than I
intended.... They're no doubt searching for you by now,
Marveaux, we have to make better time, or—What's
this? Why won't my arm move? *(He notices for first time
that his arm dangles at his side.)* Help! I must have slept
on it. Ah yes, I can feel the blood returning to it
now...and it hurts.... Right. Good. Now, Marveaux,
to it then! *(He bends down to pick up his rifle and screams
in pain and clutches his side. He collapses to the ground
again in pain; and through clenched teeth—)* I must have
slept on a stone, or stick, or both, or a nail, or all three,
when I wasn't sleeping on my arm.... Sleep, like
everything else, is not for the weak...but no matter,
we need to hurry...I see it is already the hour of sunrise,
for the water of the lake beyond is iridescent by the
growing ray that falls aslant its surface.... *(Near tears)*
The beauty of it.... Yes, continue on, Marveaux—
all the world is waking!

(We hear birdsong, cowbells, the buzz of bees, etc. and music)

MARVEAUX: Listen—you can hear the corncrake,
and the wood-pigeon, and also the golden bullfinch....
But wait, I hear something else too...sssshh...behind the
rustling of the leaves...

(We hear the rustling of the leaves....And then, softly, a mysterious and beautiful music, and faint words beautifully spoken....)

PHILOMEL: *(Unseen)* ...this result has been attained in "His Master's Voice" laboratories by the application of an entirely new scientific principle of sound amplification... The Gramophone Company Limited, Hayes, Middlesex...Middlesex...Middlesex...

(A swell of music, the words fade to a repeated whispering, and then we hear only the rustling of leaves again. MARVEAUX, moved, equanimity shattered—)

MARVEAUX: ...it was nothing... just the wind....Press on, Marveaux, our life depends on it—*(He begins to step—)* Oh God—*(Then crumples to the ground)*—and yet I cannot...Not with my heart shivering with an intensity unprecedented in the entire history of man. No, I have to find the source of that sound. Done then.

GOAT: He can almost hear it still, the sound, and the sound, so lovely, that all he can do is sing of it... Tenor with Strings.

(And MARVEAUX props himself up, buttons his jacket , etc., in preparation to leave, and sings, stirringly, in pained and earnest voice, akin to John McCormack.)

MARVEAUX: The sun is up, the lark is soaring
Loud swells the voice of chanticleer
But louder still, my heart assures
My love is near, My Love is Near,
My love...is...near....

But if I find still miles are mine
to go, then I will here attest—
That until I find my heart's one aim
I'll never rest, I'll Never REST
I Will Never.... Rest!
(He is about to set off, when he suddenly decides to attempt a

more beautiful and gentle ending)
Oh!... Never...never... Rest...
(But instead of ending there, he attempts an even more
beautifully gentle ending)
...Oh!...never...never...rest...
(Gentler, quieter, and still more lovely)
...oh...never...never...

(We hear only snoring, as MARVEAUX *has lulled himself to*
sleep. Birds and forest sounds. Lights out on all but GOAT.*)*

GOAT: Well. That did us a world of good. And we
learned how Marveaux endures being awake. By going
back to sleep, that's how. Very edifying. I shall make a
note in my conductor's logbook. *(A sudden panic)* ...But
what if I'm not a tramcar conductor, what then? I'm not
so high on my self as to think I might be a uneycorn,
loveliest creature there is. But I'm not so morose as
to think I'm something repugnant either. A goat, for
instance. Very few have seen a unicorn. But all that
do weep for the beauty of it....They're kin to the goat,
you know, unicorns, although it's hard to reckon,
impossible, how the lovely and the repulsive can be kin.
(The pain flares up another notch, and the GOAT *cries and*
bleats out) Baah!... It's worse. And why? Where am I?
Why is there nothing around? And it hurts! I don't
want this, I can't I can't, I don't want this—

(But he and we have begun to hear a soothing voice, of a
young man, and it quiets him down—)

MACMANN: *(In darkness, softly)* ...sshhh...I am here....
I will never abandon you....You are loved....I am here....
I will never abandon you....You are loved....

GOAT: Who can that be? Do you hear that? It can't be
Marveaux—

(Lights up and down on MARVEAUX, *sleeping)*

GOAT: —he's asleep.*(Pause)* Thinks. It must be
somebody else....Thinks. *(Thinks, then decisively—)*
It is Macmann.

(Lights up, and music with a flourish, to reveal MACMANN,
*hale young man, rosy cheeked, perhaps resembling a young
John McCormack, jacket, tie, and trousers circa 1910.
He kneels by the* GOAT. *We hear, faintly, a gramophone
record on order of* I'll Take You Home Kathleen*)*

GOAT: I remember now. Sounds. From a box, in
a cottage. That's the cottage I must have lived in.
A mother, that's what I was. Not a tramcar conductor
at all, but a mother, ailing, on a cot. There are worse
things than being a mother ailing on a cot. Just to name
one—goat. Lousy life, a goat's. Stretching his tether
til his neck nearly snaps and still only able to peer
in through the window at all that loveliness inside.
An ailing mother, snug by the fire. Much better.
And listening to lovely sounds from a wooden box—
O Lovely Box! Would you believe it—inside the box,
men were conversing prettily with the moon! And
loving their mothers. There's Macmann all over for you.
There's no better man than Macmann. And this too—
he loves his mother.

(Lights have come up to reveal MACMANN's MOTHER,
coughing, ailing, on a cot. GOAT *bleats bleakly. We hear rain.*
MACMANN *has tied the* GOAT *to a post, then kneels by*
MOTHER's *bedside. A makeshift desk is next to the cot)*

MACMANN: *(To* MOTHER*)* I am here...I will never
abandon you....You are loved....

MOTHER: Leave me alone.

MACMANN: My crow, you're awake.

MOTHER: I was never asleep.

MACMANN: And how are you then this newly-minted
morn?

MOTHER: Worse.

MACMANN: Nonsense. How much better you look.
You'll be out of this bed soon enough—

MOTHER: Aye, and in my grave—

MACMANN: Ho ho, listen to you. Now drink this tea
while it's hot. Ah my sweet mother—

MOTHER: Did you kill the goat?

MACMANN: I tried. I couldn't.

MOTHER: You truly are worthless. Not a penny we'll get
for him now.

MACMANN: We'll be alright.

MOTHER: O we'll be alright all right. After we starve to
death.

MACMANN: We're not going to starve. You're forgetting
I have my head.

MOTHER: Tis true. So full of oats it is, we'll never go
hungry.

MACMANN: Mother, fie. What did the doctor say.

MOTHER: I don't need a doctor, I need a chamberpot.

MACMANN: There's a modern privy now, installed and
everything.

MOTHER: The privy is broken.

MACMANN: Broken?

MOTHER: Again.

MACMANN: Hmm. An interesting problem in physics.

MOTHER: The privy is broken and backed up, nothing
could be simpler. The only problem in physics is how
I managed to give birth to such a worthless son.

MACMANN: Because of the inferiority of the plumbing, the elevated situation of our cottage, and the gradient of the piping from Roundwood reservoir, the cistern only fills halfway, and so never flushes properly. A common problem in the area apparently.

MOTHER: You're the dullest boy in the world.

MACMANN: But wouldn't that be wonderful mother? To devise a device that allowed a commode to flush effectively when the cistern is only half full?

MOTHER: And you're the boy to do it, I suppose.

MACMANN: And won't you be proud of me then, when my name's attached to every privy in Ireland!

MOTHER: Sad for this mother who knows she can't even wish for that! Now go to sleep if you're going to start your dreaming again.

MACMANN: But I only just awoke.

MOTHER: Look outside! You slept the whole day away, again.

MACMANN: The days must be getting shorter.

MOTHER: Oh you'll be the death of me.

MACMANN: I was up all night you see—

MOTHER: Doing god knows what.

MACMANN: For the millionth time, I've told you, it's the only time I have...to work.... We can't live like this forever mother...in obscurity and dreary monotony... Mother, I want to leave something lasting...something that endures in the heart of humanity...I want to be an inventor.

MOTHER: Oh, not that talk again—

MACMANN: An inventor, a famous inventor!

MOTHER: We're too poor—

MACMANN: Aye, we're poor—And yet others have
endured hardships far worse, and they persevered,
and the world wept tears of gratitude when their gifts
were unveiled...I want that....I want what Archimedes
had that cloudless day, leaping out of his bath and
running down the city street, an old man...naked...
and shouting... "Eureka...I have found it..." I want that.
And with patience, and faith, I'll have it.

MOTHER: You'll have it all right if you start running
down the street naked and shouting your head off—

MACMANN: Oh just you wait—

MOTHER: Now look here my addled one, what
materials do you have after all? What can come of it?
A few scraps of paper, a piece of string—

(MACMANN *leaps upon a chair*)

MACMANN: And what wonders have been
accomplished with less! Mother, all it takes is faith...
the Faith that helps you see what isn't readily apparent...
I haven't much, I know, but I needn't much—look at
Edison—a tin can, a sewing needle, a piece of rubber—
the phonograph! I will create nothing less than a world,
with bits of string and small scraps of paper!

(MACMANN *kisses his mother, and brushes the hair from her
face. A moment of silent love between them. Then—*)

MACMANN: Now go to sleep.

MOTHER: What about you? What are you doing.

MACMANN: I'm putting on my brown "working" jacket.
I have to stay up to work, you see, but you my crow,
to sleep...to sleep.... *(Sings—)*
The stars...so far...away....
One day will be near enough to touch....
Our life...of strife...we'll flee....
And soon...will be just a memory....

For the things are dearly few on earth
That wishes can attain
Whate'er we want of any worth
We've got to work to gain....

But O, your child is here...
So banish care and fear...
And sleep my dear... My darling...Mother of Mine!
(But instead of ending, he attempts a more gentle and beautiful final line) Oh! My darling...mother...of...mine...
(And still more beautiful)
Oh! ...My darling...mother...of mine...mine....
(And still more beautiful) ...Oh! ...my
darling...mothe—...of...

(We hear MACMANN *snoring as he has lulled himself to sleep.)*

MOTHER: Miserable boy.

(Pause. The sun rises. A cock crows)

MOTHER: Hey. You. Wake up. Tis morning.

MACMANN: What? Morning already?

MOTHER: The night is kind to those who can sleep.

MACMANN: Mother, I've told you before—inventors often get ideas when their sleeping. In that way, it was a "working" sleep. Twas anything but restful.

MOTHER: You're a big oil painting entitled "The Worthless Boy." Now get along or you'll be late for school.

MACMANN: For what?

MOTHER: Tis a school day.

MACMANN: O I couldn't leave you.

MOTHER: We don't want the truant officer round again do we now? Besides, I prefer it when you're gone.

MACMANN: Make no mistake, O world—she loves me like only a mother can!

MOTHER: Now bugger off. And take something to eat for lunch.

MACMANN: No, no lunch for me. There'd be none left for you.

MOTHER: I'm telling you, I couldn't keep it down if I tried.

MACMANN: I'll take this apple, and leave the rest.

MOTHER: Fine.

MACMANN: And a bit of bread and cheese is all. The rest we'll leave for you.

MOTHER: Fine.

MACMANN: And this potato's past bad I think. You won't be missing this.

MOTHER: I won't be missing you neither. Now get out.

MACMANN: A single slice of meat and mustard, for the teacher, and I'm off. I'm off!

MOTHER: I know, I can smell it.

MACMANN: I'll just wrap this blanket tighter—

MOTHER: To smother me—

MACMANN: And I'm off!

MOTHER: Fine.

MACMANN: So I'll kiss your sweet lips and say goodbye.

MOTHER: Leave already.

MACMANN: *(Sings)* Good...bye... Good...bye!
(He exits the cottage,)

MOTHER: And don't come back til you've killed the goat!

MACMANN: *(To* GOAT, *with somber earnestness)* Make
no mistake, she loves me...and her fits and furies are
common to all who are vulnerable from the infirmities
of age or disease, or both.... But she'll get better, and all
will be better, I know it will.

*(We hear rumbling of the approaching tram and the ringing
of its bell)*

MACMANN: Ah, and here's the tram. *(Hugs* GOAT,
then he hops aboard) Goodbye dear Goat.

GOAT: Now O Lovely Tram! Take him to a scene of
Great Beauty. Past the schoolhouse.

MACMANN: Not today you wretched building!

GOAT: And onward.

MACMANN: To the very end of the line!

GOAT: At full throttle my inner world is working.
Watch him striding off the tram and into the bright,
green meadow, and beyond.

MACMANN: To the lake.

GOAT: Lovely lovely lake.

MACMANN: It is midday I see, for the water of the lake
is iridescent by the splendent ray of noontime that falls
aslant its surface.

*(*MACMANN *has with him a fishing line.)*

GOAT: A bluebird whistles.... A glowworm rests on the
bank.

MACMANN: *(Picking up glowworm)* Hello glowworm.

GOAT: A man of nature, Macmann is.

MACMANN: *(Gently)* I'm going to have to thread the
length of you on this hook for bait. *(He threads the
glowworm on the hook and casts into the water. He lies
down on the bank.)* "The heights by great men reached

and kept, were not attained by sudden flight, but they, while their companions slept, were toiling upward in the night."

(A flourish of music and birdsong and MACMANN, *at lake, falls asleep. A* TRUANT OFFICER *appears, panting from efforts. He is a decrepit old man played by the same actor who is the voice of* GOAT.*)*

TRUANT OFFICER: So so so. There you are.

MACMANN: Oh leave me alone.

TRUANT OFFICER: You're becoming harder and harder for this truant officer to find. But one thing is for sure—when I find you, I know I'll find you asleep.

MACMANN: That's how solutions to inventions often come.

TRUANT OFFICER: Your only invention, Macmann, will be your own misery if you don't go to school.

MACMANN: I won't endure the nonsense of that school willingly—they do nothing but beat me.

TRUANT OFFICER: Well, I'll say this.... Of all the places I've had to ferret you out from, this is the loveliest— the towering stands of elm, and larch—

MACMANN: *(Pointing to—)* The hornbeam—

TRUANT OFFICER: *(Pointing)* The silver birch—

MACMANN: *(Pointing)* The Huntingdon willow—

TRUANT OFFICER: *(Pointing)*The common Laburnum—

MACMANN: *(Clenching fist)* And two ready fists, for I'm not going back without a fight.

TRUANT OFFICER: I'm sick sore and tired of fighting you, Macmann. Why can't you ever come along without the trials attached?

MACMANN: I'm as weary of this struggle as you...
(Upon rising, he has dropped a packet of cigarettes.)

TRUANT OFFICER: What's this then? A packet of
cigarettes? Won't your mother be happy to hear
about this little find—

MACMANN: Please don't tell her—twould give her
unspeakable grief!

TRUANT OFFICER: Poor as you are, your mother ailing,
and it's this you spend your pennies on?

MACMANN: I only buy them for the cigarette cards
inside. I'm collecting the whole series— "Great Men
of Science."

TRUANT OFFICER: And so you say, but you're a great
fat liar— "Great Men of Science" was put out two
summers ago by Ogden's Cigarettes, it's last year's
rubbish now. They're currently onto a lovely series—
"Flora and Fauna of Great Britain."

MACMANN: If you know your cigarette cards so well,
I hope you know the Franklyn Davies series on Boxing
poses, because I'm about to lead with a right uppercut
to knock your head off.

TRUANT OFFICER: The day you defeat me is the day I'll
leave you be.

MACMANN: Do you swear it?

TRUANT OFFICER: I do.

MACMANN: Then at last I'll have the time I need—
to work, to invent, O blessed day!—and imminent...
for I know I'm growing stronger and you, feebler—

TRUANT OFFICER: Our fights have lasted longer, tis true,
we're nearly even in strength, but until I'm bested I'll
fight you with every bit of mustard I've got and see that
you're back in that schoolhouse.

MACMANN: Come at me then!

(MACMANN and TRUANT OFFICER fight. It is an even match. The fight is long and arduous. A not-very-pretty fight, full of rolling about on the ground, into the lake, knocking over bits of the fragile set, etc.)

TRUANT OFFICER: I hate this.

MACMANN: Give up?

TRUANT OFFICER: Not I, Peter Pretty.

(More fighting, More rolling about on ground)

MACMANN: This is hell.

TRUANT OFFICER: So you're giving up, are you?

MACMANN: Nay!

(More fighting)

TRUANT OFFICER: A game of chess could have solved this just as tidily—

MACMANN: If you think I like fighting an old man—

TRUANT OFFICER: If you don't , you certainly hide it well enough—

MACMANN: I'm fighting for my freedom—

TRUANT OFFICER: No you aren't, Billy-Bentie—you're letting out through your fists all the sorrows over your ailing mother, all the frustrations that rise from your unspeakable poverty—

MACMANN: *(Near tears, sincerely hopeful)* So you don't think I'm just a delinquent?

TRUANT OFFICER: *(Sincerely)* No, Macmann...I don't....

(In a clinch, all their grunting stops, and we hear more clearly the wind rustling the leaves and the bluebird's song—a strange lull and peace. Quietly, in clinch—)

TRUANT OFFICER: We will remember this day.... This moment when our strength was evenly matched. The bluebird whistled.

(We hear the tranquil whistling of a bird.)

TRUANT OFFICER: And a lake, achingly beautiful, shivered in the fresh spring breeze. Our sleeves rolled up. Sweat on our faces... The sun will never seem so bright again. Our days will grow dimmer and dimmer, but in our darkest moment, we will remember this.... A moment more and it will pass....

(A moment. Then suddenly, the moment passes, MACMANN swings with violence, and they both struggle again. Amidst grunts and whatnot, the fighting becomes still more violent and committed, but MACMANN gains the upper hand. He has the truant officer on the ground and kicking him)

MACMANN: *(Foot cocked)* And now a kick to the windpipe to make you silent as a librarian.

TRUANT OFFICER: I've had enough.

MACMANN: Swear... Swear this sweet news.

TRUANT OFFICER: I swear.... Just stop with the kicking... It hurts.

(Just then, there is a tug on the fishing line. They both see it.)

MACMANN: Did you see that?

TRUANT OFFICER: You mean the tug on your fishing line?

MACMANN: Holy Saint Martin, I've hooked something.

(MACMANN runs to line)

TRUANT OFFICER: I can't get up.

MACMANN: Rest then, I can do it.

TRUANT OFFICER: The slack.

MACMANN: I see the slack.

TRUANT OFFICER: Take in the slack.

MACMANN: *(As he's wrestling with the fishing line, to* TRUANT OFFICER*)* I know what I'm doing.... You stay out of it.

TRUANT OFFICER: I'm just saying, the slack—

MACMANN: *(As he's reeling in)* I heard you the first time.

TRUANT OFFICER: A taut line is a fisherman's friend.

MACMANN: You stay on the ground, like a good old man.

TRUANT OFFICER: *(Getting up slowly)* Not with all that slack, I can't.

MACMANN: You know what this is, don't you? A confirmation... My life has changed, beginning now!

TRUANT OFFICER: Oh you're exultant, are you?

MACMANN: It's going to be quite a fish.... It's nearly at the bank, help me pull it out—

(They at last pull up the line, but to their surprise, it isn't a fish at the end of the line at all, but a corpse)

MACMANN: *(Sobered)* My god... A corpse...

TRUANT OFFICER: Aye, a corpse. Half-rotted away.

MACMANN: ...and half-devoured by fishes.

TRUANT OFFICER: Already the clouds are covering the sky, and what once was a caressing breeze now brings a chill....

MACMANN: Who could he be?

TRUANT OFFICER: *(Shrugging)* Nobody... Such a lake is littered with corpses.

MACMANN: But how did he drown?

TRUANT OFFICER: How indeed.

MACMANN: Fell out of his boat when he was fishing, perhaps.

TRUANT OFFICER: Perhaps... Or a cramp got the better of him while swimming.

MACMANN: Or his leg got caught in the brack.

TRUANT OFFICER: Or he was pulled down by the undertow.

MACMANN: Or an eel.

TRUANT OFFICER: Sure, or perhaps like in the stories, he was lured to his death by a Siren.

MACMANN: A Siren?

TRUANT OFFICER: Have you never heard of men sent to drowning thanks to the Siren's song?

MACMANN: No.

TRUANT OFFICER: Well you never go to school.

MACMANN: How can you drown for a song?

TRUANT OFFICER: Answer me this, Macmann— When the thing you want and love is unattainable, what then? Will you swim out to it, knowing you'll drown in the trying?

MACMANN: All I can do is try.

TRUANT OFFICER: And when you fail in the trying?

MACMANN: I'll try again.

TRUANT OFFICER: And when you fail at that?

MACMANN: I'll learn from the trying, and try again. All the world is built on trial and error. I'll never give up.

TRUANT OFFICER: Listen to this then. Are you seated comfortably? Good. We'll begin. A Scene of Great Beauty. A man, Marveaux. Asleep.

(*Lights up on* MARVEAUX *asleep.*)

TRUANT OFFICER: Lovely. But a shrew, with his sharp claw, in his haste to build his nest before the winter, pierces the sleeping Marveaux in the backside.

(MARVEAUX *awakes with a start and a scream. Pause*)

TRUANT OFFICER: And also a stabbing pain in the head.

MARVEAUX: (*Screaming again from stabbing pain in head*) I'm up, it hurts! I'm awake! Good. No more sleep. (*He takes a step, yells out in pain, and falls to ground. He thrusts hand in boot and pulls out a small knife*) My knife. I had forgotten I put it there. I should hold on to it. Good. On then... And yet...is there something I've forgotten? ...Wait....sssh...

(*We hear, faintly, the same mysterious strain of music and voice he heard before (offstage)*)

PHILOMEL: Clark Clamps for Individual Insulators— made for all pin type insulators. For details, Send for Bulletin 24. New for 1918, cleat type insulators....

MARVEAUX: (*As the voice fades*) There it is...that sound I heard before.... And try as I might, I can't banish it from my mind or heart...sssh...it seems to be coming from beyond this foliage...from the middle of the lake itself... (*And he takes a few steps, then parts the foliage leading to the lake. He freezes.*) It can't be...

GOAT: Swan's Soap! I remember! It was on a label. For a cake of Swan's Soap. Saw it briefly. The label. Won't ever forget it. It didn't belong on a rubbish heap. Too Lovely it was. And here it is.

(*A flourish of music, and a pool of light reveals a mermaid, wearing glasses, on a rock, in the midst of the lake, with a book in one hand, a bar of soap held up in the other*)

MARVEAUX: O Marveaux...you have left one dream only to step into another. For surely in the middle of this

lake achingly beautiful there sits a mermaid on a rock....
Can it be true?

PHILOMEL: Yes, it's true.

MARVEAUX: Oh god! The pain! *(He doubles over and coughs wretchedly.)*

PHILOMEL: Are you ill?

MARVEAUX: I'm shivering with fever. My veins carry not blood but a stream of razors.

PHILOMEL: What is it?

MARVEAUX: *(Spellbound and moved to tears)* Love. Tell me your name...please...so that I may know what to say as I lay dying, from this love that is shattering my heart.

PHILOMEL: Can I trust you with my name? Only those with a pure love may know it.

MARVEAUX: All I know is that there is pain, and therefore Love. I ask you, I beg you, for your name....

PHILOMEL: Philomel.

MARVEAUX: *(Tears)* Philomel...now I know all my life has led me to this moment...and I must, must know how I can win your love.

PHILOMEL: But Marveaux, you have already won it.

MARVEAUX: What words are these?

PHILOMEL: Merely the truth.

MARVEAUX: It can't be.

PHILOMEL: But now you weep.

MARVEAUX: I don't deserve it.

PHILOMEL: Yes you do...you are a great man.

MARVEAUX: What have I done?

PHILOMEL: You have endured.

MARVEAUX: And what now?

PHILOMEL: Come to me Marveaux.

MARVEAUX: What I've been through—

PHILOMEL: And now rest is yours.

MARVEAUX: I haven't slept in days— Such trials—

PHILOMEL: Now forgotten... Come to me, Marveaux...
let me hold you in my arms.

MARVEAUX: Yes...yes...I will come....

(Healthy pause)

PHILOMEL: You hesitate?

MARVEAUX: I can't help noticing the series of violently
swirling eddies and whirlpools separating me and you.

PHILOMEL: Sweet Marveaux, the eddies are there for a
reason, to protect me from those who proclaim their
love falsely. But know that if you truly love me—

MARVEAUX: I do!

PHILOMEL: —then the eddies will dissipate and all will
be calm.

MARVEAUX: Then here I come! *(Pause)* Mind you, it's
quite a swim, what with those eddies.

PHILOMEL: Look at me once more, Marveaux—with
absolute faith in me—look at me, and by this look,
you will entrust to me with absolute confidence your
entire fate.

MARVEAUX: I'm looking at you. My fate is yours.

PHILOMEL: Then come to me.

MARVEAUX: If it weren't for those swirling eddies—

PHILOMEL: Hang the eddies, you have to trust me.

MARVEAUX: I do trust you. But mind you, the swirling eddies—

PHILOMEL: And I tell you that the eddies will calm if your love is true. Now swim out, and I will be yours.

MARVEAUX: Yes, I will! *(To self)* But Marveaux, you shudder. And why? ...Because you have no proof. You can only trust her.... Down and down I'd sink... down where flatfish lay. Flatfish, and kelp....

PHILOMEL: Marveaux?

MARVEAUX: I stare into the eddies and can see only my death.

PHILOMEL: You look upon a mermaid, is that not miraculous enough for you? What future miracles are not possible?

MARVEAUX: What you say, so true...and yet... *(Shattered)* I can't...my god...I can't do it.

PHILOMEL: Then leave.

MARVEAUX: No! Please!

PHILOMEL: You shall never see me or this lake again.

MARVEAUX: I can't! ...I can't walk away from love.... But I cannot swim towards it either...it hurts.... Even a dead, stuffed goat, revived again to a sort of life by a pain unspeakable, cannot begin to imagine my torment.

PHILOMEL: But if you won't come to me, and you won't leave—

MARVEAUX: —Then what can I do? But stay here until my eyesight dims and I can say to myself at last, "you see, Marveaux, it is not what you thought was on that rock. It is merely a shrub, or a seal—

PHILOMEL: Or a manatee.

MARVEAUX: —It is not a thing of beauty...With eyes finally dim, I will convince myself you are nothing I might have loved.

PHILOMEL: You know nothing about love...

GOAT: Day turns to night. Frogs hop.

(Pitch dark. Frog croak. Very long pause. Then, still in dark—)

PHILOMEL: Are you still there?

MARVEAUX: Yes I am.... *(Pause)* Philomel?

PHILOMEL: What.

MARVEAUX: What is a manatee?

PHILOMEL: Go to sleep.

GOAT: An evening shower. Drenches all. Then dawn and then—

(Lights up)

PHILOMEL: *(Looking up from her reading)* You're still here.

MARVEAUX: Surely I impress you with my constancy.

PHILOMEL: You impress me with your cowardice.

MARVEAUX: So long as I impress you somehow.... *(Pause)* Philomel...if mermaids exist, then surely unicorns exist as well. Have you ever seen one?

PHILOMEL: I saw one very briefly.

MARVEAUX: Did you!?

PHILOMEL: It was in an advertisement for a bicycle pump.

MARVEAUX: Ah. But in real life—

PHILOMEL: There's no such thing as unicorns.

MARVEAUX: How can you be so sure? A goat with a horn—

PHILOMEL: It isn't a goat with a horn, it's a horse with a horn, and I'm telling you they don't exist. There's nothing more fatuous than all that fairy-tale piffle.

MARVEAUX: How funny coming from a mermaid.

(Pause, no response as PHILOMEL *continues to read)*

MARVEAUX: I said, that sounds awfully fu—

PHILOMEL: I heard you.

MARVEAUX: They say only a virgin can capture a unicorn.

PHILOMEL: Will you keep quiet.

(Pause. She reads her book.)

MARVEAUX: Wouldn't that be a sight—a mermaid capturing a unicorn!

PHILOMEL: *(Losing patience)* But I *can't* capture a unicorn!

MARVEAUX: What do you mean—surely you're a virgin—

PHILOMEL: I mean there's *no such thing as unicorns.*

MARVEAUX: Philomel—you haven't had any lovers before me, have you?

PHILOMEL: *(Erupting)* Can't you see I'm trying to read?

GOAT: This all began so well.

MARVEAUX: This all began so well. But I've made a hash of it.

GOAT: A new man. Try that. Call him...Halliwell.

(Lights up to reveal HALLIWELL, *thin mustache, dressed smartly in a W W I uniform)*

HALLIWELL: Marveaux, there are tears in my eye upon seeing you again.

MARVEAUX: Halliwell? Can it truly be? ...I thought I'd never see you again!

HALLIWELL: Marveaux... My old childhood chum.

MARVEAUX: Oh what sweet luck! What are the chances of us meeting like this? It must be fate.

HALLIWELL: Words like "fate" are a lot of applesauce. I've been looking for you.

MARVEAUX: But why my friend?

HALLIWELL: You know very well why.

MARVEAUX: Do I?

HALLIWELL: Yes you do.

MARVEAUX: Really?

HALLIWELL: Yes.

MARVEAUX: Do I owe you money?

HALLIWELL: As a matter of fact, you do. But I'm not going to tramp through forests and mud for that.

MARVEAUX: Then what then?

HALLIWELL: Have you forgotten Belgium?

MARVEAUX: Belgium?

HALLIWELL: Your comrades haven't forgotten Belgium—everyday in the field they remember Belgium as they go over the top, as they make corpses out of the Hun and watch the Hun return the favour.

MARVEAUX: Oh. Belgium.

HALLIWELL: Yes, Belgium. You abandoned your countrymen in the midst of battle, Marveaux. I've been sent to find you, and bring you back.

MARVEAUX: Back?

HALLIWELL: Yes.

MARVEAUX: You?

HALLIWELL: I hadn't a choice.

MARVEAUX: But friend, don't you know that they execute all who desert the field?

HALLIWELL: That's not always the case.

MARVEAUX: Yes it is.

HALLIWELL: No it isn't.

MARVEAUX: Oh god! It is! Look, look—you have to pretend you never saw me.

HALLIWELL: If they hear that I let you go, it'll be *me* against the wall.

MARVEAUX: *(A plea)* But our friendship!

HALLIWELL: Yes, our Friendship! Imagine how I felt, trained in tracking errant soldiers only to hear that my next task was to find the deserter Marveaux!

MARVEAUX: But how did you find me?

HALLIWELL: Are you kidding? The battle rages not a half mile from here. Why for god's sake have you not put more distance between you and the army since you bolted?

MARVEAUX: Her.

(MARVEAUX *points out* PHILOMEL *in the middle of the lake.)*

HALLIWELL: *(Lighting a cigarette)* Ah, I see.... And who might this ravishing young fish be?

MARVEAUX: Her name is Philomel. If I can swim out to her, she's mine.

HALLIWELL: But you'll sink like a stone. Can't you see those eddies?

MARVEAUX: Of course I can. They're there to protect her from unpure love. They'll dissipate if my love—

HALLIWELL: Friend, get a hold of yourself! Can't you see this thing is a Siren?

MARVEAUX: You only just met her—How do you know she's a siren?

HALLIWELL: All women are sirens. *(Exasperated)* Why did you abandon the field in the first place?!

MARVEAUX: I didn't believe in the cause.

HALLIWELL: You mean you didn't want to be killed.

MARVEAUX: For the cause.

PHILOMEL: Are there causes you would die for?

MARVEAUX: Only love is worth fighting for.

PHILOMEL: You would sacrifice yourself for love?

MARVEAUX: If I had to.

PHILOMEL: Then swim out to me.

HALLIWELL: *(Doubtful)* Yes, swim out to her.

MARVEAUX: I will. *(Pause)* Soon.

PHILOMEL: You're a coward.

MARVEAUX: Halliwell—

HALLIWELL: She's right—you're a coward.

MARVEAUX: Throughout the ages, men have spoken of the mermaid, and the bliss that can be attained by finding her.

HALLIWELL: Yes, but they were drunk.

MARVEAUX: But here she sits!

PHILOMEL: You don't seem very impressed, Halliwell.

HALLIWELL: Sorry sister.

PHILOMEL: Perhaps you've seen a mermaid before?

HALLIWELL: The only mermaid I ever saw was on the label of a bar of soap.

PHILOMEL: Was she attractive?

HALLIWELL: She wasn't my type.

PHILOMEL: Am I more your type?

HALLIWELL: You're about the same.

PHILOMEL: You should buy soap with chorus girls on the label.

HALLIWELL: You certainly have me pegged, don't you.

PHILOMEL: I bet you spend a good deal of time thinking about chorus girls.

HALLIWELL: And soap. I'm a great believer in the things that keep a man civilized.

PHILOMEL: The Eskimos are eaters of soap.

HALLIWELL: So you've met an Eskimo, have you?

PHILOMEL: I've never left the lake. But books I've had.

HALLIWELL: What's that you're reading now.

PHILOMEL: The February 1917 issue of *Electrical World*.

HALLIWELL: That's pretty dry reading for the mermaid type.

PHILOMEL: What would you have me read?

HALLIWELL: I don't know, what are the other girls reading—romances,—

PHILOMEL: Nothing's half as vapid or insipid as a romance.

HALLIWELL: There! Now tell me honestly, Marveaux—is that the girl for you?

MARVEAUX: It makes her only more mysterious.

HALLIWELL: All right then—one more question, Phyllis—where did you scare up that particular periodical when you're stuck in the middle of a lake?

PHILOMEL: From the clutches of the corpse of a drowned electrical engineer.

HALLIWELL: Do you mind my asking how he drowned?

PHILOMEL: By swimming in my general direction through swirling eddies and raging whirlpools that proved too daunting for him.

HALLIWELL: Electrical engineers as a breed are pretty scrawny.

PHILOMEL: Yes they certainly are.

HALLIWELL: But I'd bet you ten to one that my father, who used to do a hundred laps at the club without batting an eye, couldn't make it a minute in those whirlpools of yours.

PHILOMEL: I don't believe in betting.

HALLIWELL: You're asking my friend here to bet his life. And at lousy odds.

MARVEAUX: *(To* PHILOMEL*)* Don't listen to him.

HALLIWELL: Keep quiet.

MARVEAUX: Odds are set without ever taking account for love, which is the Great Enabler, and Faith, which transcends statistics and reason.

PHILOMEL: He's right.

HALLIWELL: *(To* PHILOMEL*)* Love and Faith?! How many men have drowned swimming to you?

PHILOMEL: After a thousand, I couldn't be bothered to count.

HALLIWELL: And yet you expect our Marveaux here to put on his trunks and do his best Trudgen stroke out to you all the same.

PHILOMEL: Marveaux—you aren't like the others.

MARVEAUX: *(To* HALLIWELL*)* Did you hear that?

HALLIWELL: *(To* MARVEAUX*)* It's true, you're not like the others. You're the greatest coward this world has ever seen. And it may have put you in some pretty hot water with HQ, but at least it saved your neck here with what's her name—Frank something.

MARVEAUX: *(Correcting)* Philomel. *(To* PHILOMEL*)* And don't listen to him. Go on—how am I not like the others?

PHILOMEL: By this fact alone...I love you.

MARVEAUX: O Philomel, If only you knew how my heart aches upon hearing those words—

HALLIWELL: *(To* PHILOMEL*)* Why don't you swim to *him* then.

MARVEAUX: *(To* HALLIWELL*)* Keep out of this—

HALLIWELL: A flick of your tail and you'd be in his arms in no time.

PHILOMEL: You're missing the point.

HALLIWELL: Okay, look, I'm not going to stand around here all day. You're coming with me.

MARVEAUX: You'll have to shoot me first.

HALLIWELL: I'm not going to shoot you.

PHILOMEL: Why not?

HALLIWELL: *(To* PHILOMEL*)* Because I love him like a brother, even if he does give me a headache.

PHILOMEL: Then you're as much a coward as he is.

HALLIWELL: Call me what you will. But do you see this gun? *(He takes out his service revolver. Then throws it into the lake)* Now you're coming with me, Marveaux. Am I going to need these cuffs on you?

MARVEAUX: No...I'll go quietly.

HALLIWELL: That's my boy.

(But just as HALLIWELL *and* MARVEAUX *begin to walk off,* MARVEAUX *dives for his rifle with bayonet attached and points it at* HALLIWELL. *Pause.)*

HALLIWELL: Putting the rifle down—that's what I suggest.

MARVEAUX: And you call yourself a friend.

HALLIWELL: Don't you know I was given orders to kill you if you gave me resistance? Why do you think I volunteered to find you? To make sure some trigger-happy artillery man didn't shoot you as soon as he caught sight of you.

PHILOMEL: Marveaux, I know he's your friend, but surely you see there's only one way out. Shoot him and then swim to me.

HALLIWELL: That's advice we can do without. Marveaux, she's not good enough for you. And she's a fish. Her face isn't bad but she'll give you nothing but trouble. And here's some good advice—put the rifle down.

MARVEAUX: You don't understand Love. You never have.

HALLIWELL: I just don't want to see you hurt.

MARVEAUX: What do you call sending me in front of a firing squad?

HALLIWELL: Well what do you call falling in love?

MARVEAUX: One is murder!

HALLIWELL: The other's suicide!

MARVEAUX: The heart can't help what it loves.

HALLIWELL: What good is Love if it causes so much suffering?

MARVEAUX: With love, anything is bearable.

HALLIWELL: Your choice of women was always lousy.

MARVEAUX: Do I need to remind you, a woman has come between us before?

HALLIWELL: That was long ago.

MARVEAUX: Have I ever forgiven you?

HALLIWELL: Of course you have.... Surely you have.... But look, if you haven't...now's the time.

PHILOMEL: Marveaux, listen to me. I love you. I love you. Shoot him.

(Pause. MARVEAUX fires twice. But the rifle hasn't any bullets. Pause. HALLIWELL rushes MARVEAUX. MARVEAUX tries to protect himself with the bayonet, but HALLIWELL deftly wrestles it from MARVEAUX and throws the rifle away. MARVEAUX tries to flee. HALLIWELL grabs MARVEAUX. MARVEAUX lands a blow to HALLIWELL, HALLIWELL recovers and grabs MARVEAUX. They roll about on the floor in a not-very-pretty bit of wrestling—fighting, clawing, in clutches, etc. They roll offstage.)

GOAT: But mind you, there's a glowworm that's gasping on the bank of the lake, and there it is. *(A flourish of music, a dim light by bank of lake)* It was stuck on the corpse that was beached by Macmann. But did you know the worm was also half-eaten by a carp. And a trout got to it too. And it was speared by a hook, remember that? But being a glowworm, it leaves a little of its light wherever it goes. It diminishes in light, but bequeaths that light to the world. O worm, teach me how to live! *(Pause)* Or are you dead. No, see,

there, it wriggles. Mark my words, the worm's story's
the most beautiful one of them all. Now rest, o worm....
Night's a fine time. *(Pause)* Now it's too dark to see
anything..*(And indeed it is)*...but what's this...*(And a sun,
ineptly made, on a scrap of paper, begins to rise, with
beautiful music accompanying)*...the sun! ...And with it...
Light... Are those two pitted still in struggle...? There
they are....

(We see MARVEAUX *and* HALLIWELL *on the ground,
curled in each other's arms, half-asleep)*

GOAT: Are they sleeping? Not sleep, no. But resting.
In each other's arms, they rested, briefly, and otherwise
they fought through the night.

*(*HALLIWELL *and* MARVEAUX *recommence wrestling.*
MARVEAUX *at last struggles out of* HALLIWELL's *grasp.
Stands up.* HALLIWELL *rushes him.* MARVEAUX *knees*
HALLIWELL *in the groin.* HALLIWELL *doubles over but still
manages to struggle over to* MARVEAUX, *grab him, and send
a fist into his gut.* MARVEAUX *and* HALLIWELL *clutch each
other's shoulders and* MARVEAUX *again knees* HALLIWELL
squarely in the groin. This act inspires HALLIWELL, *in
terrible pain but incensed by* MARVEAUX's *tactics, to recover
quickly enough to grab* MARVEAUX *and swiftly knee him in
the groin.* MARVEAUX *doubles over and* HALLIWELL *tackles
him to the ground. However, while both are on the ground,*
MARVEAUX *knees* HALLIWELL *in the groin. This just about
knocks all the wind out of* HALLIWELL, *but he summons
up enough strength to knee* MARVEAUX *in the groin.*
MARVEAUX *attempts to crawl to his bayonet, but*
HALLIWELL *crawls over top of him and grabs the rifle,
pointing the bayonet at* MARVEAUX.*)*

HALLIWELL: Now get up you. Enough of this.

*(*MARVEAUX *gets up and* HALLIWELL *puts the handcuffs on*
MARVEAUX.*)*

HALLIWELL: This way.

(MARVEAUX *walks a few steps. Gazes with painful longing at* PHILOMEL. *Then is pushed by* HALLIWELL *to continue, and they exit. The scrap of a sun sets. A miserable scrap of a moon rises.)*

GOAT: Now dusk, and peace returns to the lake. Mermaid reads from her book. Lovely book.

PHILOMEL: *(Reading)* "The unfailing reliability of The Blackburn-Smith Enclosed Tank Switch and Assembly offers service heretofore unobtainable."

GOAT: All is lovely and peace.

PHILOMEL: "The design and details are fully explained in our bulletin which..."

GOAT: No. All is not lovely and peace.

PHILOMEL: *(Disturbed)* How is this possible.... That I can't concentrate on my reading, when nothing before has impeded my concentration? ...How is this possible... that all seems nothing without him.... What was it about him that can make the world seem bleak and worthless now that he's gone.... It isn't possible...and yet it's empirically undeniable...that all the world is forever changed, with merely the thought of his name...Halliwell...Halliwell....

(A cock crows. The same sun, drawn on a scrap of paper, rises. Lights up slowly on a man in shadows)

PHILOMEL: *(Hopeful)* What is this? What man is this? Could it be?

(...and MARVEAUX *is revealed.* PHILOMEL *noticeably disappointed.)*

MARVEAUX: I have returned. Halliwell has let me go, and I have returned.

PHILOMEL: Swim out to me.

MARVEAUX: I can't.

PHILOMEL: Then go away.

MARVEAUX: I can't.

PHILOMEL: Then keep quiet. I have to think.

GOAT: Day turns to night. Then night turns to day.
And then day turns to night. Six hundred times this
happens. And then...seven hundred thousand times.
The bastarding sun and the bastarding moon. And
Marveaux doesn't sleep for a wink of it. He is in pain
and awake. This happens another fifty thousand times
after that. And then again.

(Cock crow, the sun rises. Then sets)

GOAT: And then one more time.

(Cock crow, the sun rises. Then sets)

GOAT: And then, wouldn't you know it, the lousy old
sun again.

MARVEAUX: May I speak?

PHILOMEL: No.

MARVEAUX: I was thinking...maybe it wouldn't be such
a bad idea if you swam to me after all...rather than my
swimming to you...

PHILOMEL: Do you know where Halliwell went?

MARVEAUX: ...Yes...but I don't see why—

PHILOMEL: *(Interrupting)* If I swam to you, would you
take me to him?

(Long pause)

MARVEAUX: ...Yes...

PHILOMEL: Then I will swim to you.

MARVEAUX: Such words! O Philomel! My Love!
But...*(Pause)*...why is it again that you want to see him?

PHILOMEL: That's not your concern.

MARVEAUX: Is it because you love him?

PHILOMEL: Yes. Will you still take me to him?

MARVEAUX: Yes.

PHILOMEL: Then you are a fool.

MARVEAUX: I am in love with you. If that makes me a
fool, then so be it....

GOAT: *(Desperate, anguished and fed up)* Enough!
Enough of this! No. Darkness on it all. I can't go on.
A punctured lung for Marveaux and tumors bloom
behind Her eyes, leave them to die, the end. They all
die. The end. And in pain. The end. It hurts, all of me
hurts, it isn't working.... And where did Macmann go?
He'd understand. He'd put the gun to my head....
That would be something. Macmann. Deliver me from
my misery.

(And lights up on MOTHER. MACMANN *enters,
disconsolate.)*

MOTHER: Deliver me from my misery.

MACMANN: The miserablelest misery is mine, all mine.

MOTHER: Is that you, Macmann?

MACMANN: What's left of me.

MOTHER: Well is it you or not? I can't see now you
know. I've gone blind.

MACMANN: No mother, never blind—the truth in your
darling eyes is ever-dawning.

MOTHER: O Lord, it's you alright. Did you just come in
from killing the goat?

MACMANN: I couldn't kill him.

MOTHER: Bloody hell—

MACMANN: But perhaps you didn't hear what I said. The miserablelest misery is mine, all mine.

MOTHER: I heard you all right.

MACMANN: Well it is.

MOTHER: And how is that then?

MACMANN: Molly's left me.

MOTHER: Who?

MACMANN: Molly. Molly Brannigan. She's gone and left me, and I'll never be a man again.

MOTHER: A man again? Did I miss the first time then?

MACMANN: It's comfort I be needing mother. Is there nothing you can say to make life worth facing again?

MOTHER: Which one is Molly? Didn't we go through this twice already with Kathleen? Or was it Peggy? Or Rosaleen. Ah no, twas Maggie—

MACMANN: Aye, they've all done me in. Mother, tell me, what's the point of Love if it leads to nothing but suffering?

MOTHER: What's the point of telling you to kill the goat if you take ten years to do it?

MACMANN: I see now there's only one who will ever be true, and that's you—you'll never leave me, mother—

MOTHER: God knows I'm trying. The doctor says it won't be long now.

MACMANN: Ah he's been saying that ever since I was a prattling, gurgling thing on your knee.

MOTHER: Aye, and if that wasn't twenty minutes ago, I don't know when it was. Ten years now since you left school for good and what have you to show for it.

MACMANN: I'm trying—

MOTHER: Well look...as I won't be here much longer, I have something for you.... *(Taking out a pouch from under the cot)* Take it.

MACMANN: What is it?

MOTHER: Just a bit of savings. Some peelings and shavings I've put away over the years. I want you to buy equipment with it.

MACMANN: What do you mean?

MOTHER: Equipment, equipment. For your science invention things.

MACMANN: You can't mean it....

MOTHER: Take it.

MACMANN: *(Tears welling, a song beginning—)* Mother... Oh mother—

MOTHER: Stop it. Just get out.

MACMANN: *(Singing)*
And if to thee I return,
oerburdened with care,
the heart's dearest solace
always smiles on me here!

MOTHER: *(Interrupting)* Stop with that racket—
Now get a move on, and buy what you need.

MACMANN: I will!

MOTHER: Then come back and fix the privy.

MACMANN: I will!

MOTHER: And one more thing—

MACMANN: I will!

MOTHER: Shoot the goat. He's got the liver rot, and the bloody flux, and—

MACMANN: He's getting better—

MOTHER: He's getting worse, and he's suffering.
The butcher won't take him, but the tanner might.
Now take him round the side and have done with it.

MACMANN: ...I will....

MOTHER: And if it's still early—

MACMANN: Yes?

MOTHER: You can come back and do the same to me.

MACMANN: Mother, fie! It's a ripe old age you'll be
living to.

MOTHER: Aye, as ripe as that thing in your head you
think with. Now go. And be back before dinner.

MACMANN: *(Singing)*
Ireland must be Heaven
For an angel came from there...
I never knew a living soul
One half as sweet or fair
Oh! Her eyes are like the Starlight,
And! the white clouds match her hair...
Sure all Ireland must be Heaven,
For! My Mother, Came...from There!

MOTHER: Sweet Mary, why couldn't you make me deaf
instead of blind!

MACMANN: *(Singing)* Goodbye! ...Good...bye!

(The mother throws a shoe from her cot at MACMANN *and*
MACMANN *approaches the tethered* GOAT *with musket in
hand. Amidst periodic bleating from the goat, and plaintive
music—)*

MACMANN: Come on old friend, let's...let's go for a
walk and I'll buy you...a banana.... Oh what a liar I
am.... You know where you're going, don't you boy?
It's for the best you know.... You're suffering, and we
all have our time to go.... And now it's yours.... We saw
our share of sun and storm. I'm sorry if I didn't always

keep you warm...but perhaps it wasn't all too bad....
No, none of that bleating now, you'll make us sad....
They say sunshine follows shadow, and if only that
were true—with this pouch in my pocket, it is for me,
but if only there was some way for you— *(A thought
occurs....He fishes in pocket....Pulls out a letter)* Hang on.
I just thought of something....I got this letter a week
back, sent to the wrong address... "From V Wright, the
backer's friend—29 Sweet Reasons why Blossomtime's
the Best—A shoo-in according to a man in the know—
Leopardstown Races...such and such a date—" Holy
Saint Martin, That's today! *(And as the music changes
to a promising strain—)* Oh Goat, don't you see—it's
Providence! A pouch full of savings, a timely tip,
it all adds up—and it won't be just scientific equipment,
but a whole new life for us! Fifty to one, Blossomtime
in the Third—you stay right there, I'll be right back,
and carrying a bagful of happier days with me!

GOAT: *(As* MACMANN *exits)* Thinks... How lovely for
mother to have a son like Macmann..... Thinks... How
lovely for Macmann to have a brain like Macmann's....
How lovely for horse to have a part in it all.... Thinks...

PHILOMEL: *(Distant, offstage)* There's no such thing as
unicorns.

MARVEAUX: *(Distant, offstage)* How can you be so sure?
A goat with a horn—

PHILOMEL: *(Distant, offstage)* It isn't a goat with a horn,
it's a horse with a horn...a horse with a horn....

GOAT: Thinks... I'm not so high and mighty after all as
to think I might be a uneycorn. But a horse... Why not
a horse... A racehorse...fleet-footed...chestnut colored...
Surely that's what I am. "Blossomtime." Bjesus, that
rings a bell—

*(And we hear the bell signaling the lifting of the gate at the
start of a race. We hear the roar of the crowd in the stands*

and the thundering of hooves. MACMANN, *with binoculars, is in the stands.)*

MACMANN: Run! Run!

GOAT: And I'm off! I remember clear as day. Galloping with hooves of fire, I looked neither left nor right, but straight ahead, where glory and oats awaited.... Oh lovely feeling—how wrong I was—what I thought I remembered was the rumble of the tram was really the rumble of two dozen hooves on the straightaway!

MACMANN: They're passing round the turn...here they come! Where's Blossomtime?!

GOAT: Running faster than the wind, nay! I was the wind itself! I had put so much distance between me and the rest of the pack, it wasn't even funny.

MACMANN: There he is! Oh Jesus! He's in last place! Look at all that distance between him and the rest of the pack! What are you doing! Run! Run you bastard! O you're murdering me.... Oh god! He's down! He's collapsed!

(The GOAT *tips over. And amidst the thundering of hooves, the roar of the crowd)*

MACMANN: Crawl! Crawl! You can do it!

GOAT: Oh I want to! I want to win! But it's hard going when your legs are shot to skitter.... What is it they do with racehorses with legs in splinters...I'm trying to remember....

(We suddenly hear a loud gunshot. A whinny. Another gunshot. Then silence. We see MACMANN *returning home. He rips up his racing ticket. He sees his ailing* MOTHER *inside. He grabs the musket. We hear the bleat of* GOAT. *He holds musket to head of* GOAT. *Lights out. We then hear the report of a musket. Silence. Now we hear a needle placed on a scratchy gramophone record,* I'll Take You Back,

Kathleen, *and a tableau of the* TAXIDERMIST *paying*
MACMANN *a very small sum for the* GOAT's *carcass,*
loading the carcass in a cart or barrow, and slowly carting
it to the TAXIDERMIST's *shack, where he sets* GOAT *down*
amidst other examples of his craft. Props GOAT *up. The*
TAXIDERMIST *is played by the same elderly actor who*
perhaps the TRUANT OFFICER *[And the voice of the* GOAT*].*
Now up on the sound of the wind whistling outside.)

TAXIDERMIST: *(Looking outside window, and throwing a*
blanket over himself) That's a storm all right....Even the
moon looks cold...But we're snug enough in here aren't
we...A little wisp on the fire...there we go....But I pity
the carolers, that's true. Those poor carolers! Out in
that! Imagine! *(To* GOAT *carcass)* Did you know I was a
taxidermist? Well I am. A taxidermist, living a solitary
life and talking to his carcasses for company. Do you
know what a taxidermist is? *(Now manipulating jaw of*
GOAT *so the* GOAT *can "answer"—)*
"No, I don't know what a taxidermist is. Does it
perchance have to do with the collecting of property
taxes?" Not at all. It has nothing to do with property
taxes.
"Poll taxes?" Nay.
"Sales taxes?" Oh you're not even close.
"Perhaps then the tax attached to the purchasing of
defunct biscuit works." That's called a lien tax, and
I'm telling you I have nothing to do with taxes.
"Will you then not enlighten me sir, for my
edification?" Well, since you ask so nicely, this is what
I do—I flay you, dispose of your intestines, clean your
fur, treat your skin with a preserving preparation, and
then mount you, and in that way, though dead you be,
I'll bring you all the way back again to life! Or a sort of
life. Life-like. That is, if that. No. You won't be fooling
anybody. *(Manipulating* GOAT's *jaw)*
"But tell me this sir...Is there money in it?"
Well for a carcass, you're pretty shrewd, aren't you. Is

there money in it. If you weren't a goat, if you were a
bit more rare and wondrous perhaps—
"A unicorn for instance?"
A uneycorn? Well I could retire in splendor then
couldn't I? With a stuffed unicorn. Wouldn't that be
something. But I haven't seen one and no one else has
neither. Fox, swordfish was more the line of creature
I was thinking of. But I tell you what. There *is* a bit of
money in a stuffed carcass of a goat.
"For even a goat?"
Well not much for a goat, but yes, even a goat. And we
owe it all to the greatest man that ever was.
"Was his name Macmann?"
O don't ask me. I can't remember his name.
"But what did our man do? Can you remember that?
And why he's responsible for a market in stuffed
goats?"
It's owing to the fact that the greatest of men was born
in a barn. Like you. Aye. It's true. And in a trough too.
"Very edifying. But what did he do that was so great?"
Besides being born in a barn? He suffered, man. He
suffered something fierce. He was a great one for the
suffering. He even went and suffered for every one else
too. And wasn't that a good thing for the man to do—
it's a lonely job, god knows—suffering is—but oh he
was glad to do it...glad to do it...A few more like him
and we'd be all right...And it's his birthday coming up,
and so in honor and gratitude, we make a little scene.
"A little scene?"
Aye, A little scene of Great Beauty—a barn like the
one he was borned in, and here we put the trough
containing our man, and here's his Mother, and here's
his father, and also kings, and tramcar operators and
whatnot, and last but not least—The Animals. Sheep,
hens, dogs...*goats*...and that's you...so you'll do...you'll
make us a few pennies—a botched job, but at least
you're standing.... You'll do...not in the front, mind you,

not by the trough, or by Mary, god no, but next to a
cow perhaps? Would you like that?
"I would like to be in a scene of great beauty."
Well behind a cow then...you'll fill out the scene...
you'll do that...you'll serve as you can....

(Suddenly, a knock on the door)

TAXIDERMIST: There—do you hear that?
"It sounded like a knock on the door."
Right you are. That would be the carolers...they'll tell
you all about the great man—

(The TAXIDERMIST *opens the door,* HALLIWELL *stumbles in,
near death, drenched from precipitation, and bleeding
profusely from his middle. He collapses on the floor.)*

HALLIWELL: There's a trail of blood that stretches sixty
miles over the hills...and it's mine. I saw a light in your
window. O The bogs...the wolves...but that's all over
now...I'm going to die of this wound.

TAXIDERMIST: I can help you.

HALLIWELL: *(Hopeful)* What do you mean? Are you a
doctor?

TAXIDERMIST: I'm a taxidermist.

HALLIWELL: *(Giving up completely, near-delirious
from exhaustion)* Fine, why not. Just keep it simple.
Standing's fine, or sitting, staring out, through eyes
of dark brown glass—

TAXIDERMIST: I'm not talking about mounting you—
I mean I have a needle and thread and I know how to
stitch you up and you need stitching up or you'll die.

HALLIWELL: It doesn't matter. What a horror I've been
through. The bogs, the wolves—

(The TAXIDERMIST *has fetched his tools and now cradles*
HALLIWELL *in his lap and sets to stitching.)*

TAXIDERMIST: Keep quiet, we'll see you through.
This might hurt a bit.

HALLIWELL: Did you hear what I said? Standing,
sitting, it doesn't matter, just make sure the trousers
are pressed, a cigarette in this hand, no, this hand...
forget the cigarette—make it...a banana—

TAXIDERMIST: *(Impatient)* Try to keep quiet—think about
living—

HALLIWELL: Living! He left me for dead in the woods.
My childhood friend! That bastard—

TAXIDERMIST: Quiet—there'll be time for talk—

HALLIWELL: He said he had a pebble in his boot. "Then,
take your boot off." "Well I need these cuffs off me
first," he said. So I take off the cuffs, and what do you
think—inside the boot it wasn't a pebble at all, no, it
was a knife, and he plunges it right through every one
of my organs, then runs away like a squirrel with a nut.

TAXIDERMIST: Hold still—

HALLIWELL: I'll be still soon enough.

TAXIDERMIST: You must try to live—

HALLIWELL: Why?

TAXIDERMIST: Do you have nothing to live for?

HALLIWELL: I can't think of a thing.

TAXIDERMIST: A hobby perhaps?

HALLIWELL: I'll miss the Club...the swim...the toweling
off, the shaving soap on the face...but to hell with it.

TAXIDERMIST: A loved one perhaps.

HALLIWELL: There's no such thing as love.... Here...
take off my shoes.... Or I'll take them off myself—
lay them out so I can see them—

TAXIDERMIST: Hold still—

HALLIWELL: There... And now my trousers...let me take them off—

TAXIDERMIST: No. Stop moving—

HALLIWELL: I'm taking them off!.... *(Grunts with pain)* ...Good...now I'll fold them neatly...God...have you ever seen trousers like those.

TAXIDERMIST: Sssh...be calm... Just think of breathing.

HALLIWELL: There's no reason to breathe...

TAXIDERMIST: There is! Just two more stitches, and I'll show you!

HALLIWELL: Tell the boys at the club I'm not coming back—

TAXIDERMIST: Almost done—

HALLIWELL: —Or no, I will be back..Mounted. They can stick me in the lobby—

TAXIDERMIST: Keep quiet. One more stitch—

HALLIWELL: *(Now quite delirious)* Or to hell with it... it was all a bad dream.... But that once...when he thought he had soared through the heavens...soared, ever so gently, through starfield....but no, he was mistaken...It was only a dream...There was nothing like that in this farce.... *(He nearly dies; then, breathing heavily, with wide wild eyes, glowing with beatitude—)* ...but then....after he awoke, he found a speck of stardust in his hand....it was true...he had touched...a star...

(And HALLIWELL *goes quiet. The clock strikes midnight.* HALLIWELL *has died, cradled in* TAXIDERMIST's *arms.)*

TAXIDERMIST: Dead. *(And he, with tears in his voice, sings sincerely, waveringly, and rather horribly, the following—)* Sail on...as straight as an arrow And before the morrow

In Heaven you'll Be...
And White Wings...they never grow weary
So spread out your white wings
And rest soon you'll see...

I'll...bury...you in the garden I'll...

(The song descends to a coughing, and choked up with weeping, when suddenly we hear, distant at first but growing nearer, a very slow and very beautiful rendition of Silent Night*)*

TAXIDERMIST: Christmas...it's Christmas....

(And HALLIWELL *groans back to life.)*

TAXIDERMIST: And you're alive!

HALLIWELL: I couldn't do it. Not like that.

TAXIDERMIST: You couldn't die?

HALLIWELL: No.

TAXIDERMIST: You found something lovely to live for!

HALLIWELL: I did. *(Long pause)* Revenge.

(Lights up on MOTHER *and* MACMANN*)*

MOTHER: Macmann...I know it wasn't a mint, but all those savings I gave you those years ago and all you could purchase was what again?

MACMANN: *(Feeling low and sheepish)* This bit of rubber tubing.

MOTHER: Grey rubber tubing.

MACMANN: Aye, well... It always comes in grey.... Nearly a foot of it, mind...well...eight inches at least....

MOTHER: And you're sure you didn't waste away the savings somewhere else perhaps? At the races perhaps? So you couldn't afford nothing but the tubing?

MACMANN: Well...no...that's...scientific equipment for you.... Expensive, but...quality...

MOTHER: It must be a powerful nice bit of tubing.

MACMANN: Oh aye...it's wonderful tubing.

MOTHER: And it will help now in your experiments, will it? Your tubing?

MACMANN: Oh if you only knew! It's mirac'lous what I can do now.... Now that I have...this bit of rubber tubing....

MOTHER: Glad to hear it...you miserable boy.

MACMANN: And now, just you wait.

MOTHER: There's nothing to wait for.

MACMANN: Where there's life, there's hope.

MOTHER: Where there's life, there's disappointment. And a bit of tubing. Now leave me alone.

MACMANN: No...Not on your life, my crow. My mother, my own sweet mother.

(Pause. Silence. No movement from MOTHER.*)*

MACMANN: My own sweet mother.... *(Long pause. He doesn't weep, but wipes tears from his eyes)* I'll bury you in the morning. *(He sits down at table, begins to work on inventions, then in despair and frustration, he pushes the entire table over)* Well...that's that.... Every day I thatch the roof, and every day the crows come and snatch the thatch away again for their own nests....and the rain pours in, unabated...I can't do this anymore.... *(Weeping—)* Was there ever a moment once, Once! when life seemed a blessing? Or anything other than the foul muckheap I always seem to see? No... And if that's so....do I have any choice but to kill myself. *(He makes a noose out of a bit of rope, and as he stands on a chair to drape the noose over the rafter—)* What evidence did I

have that man's acts could be noble, what proof
did I have that the world contained meaning and
beauty?...None... None at all...

*(Suddenly, distantly, we hear the birds and sounds of the
lake. They grow louder, with gentle music playing, and then
we hear the words of the* TRUANT OFFICER—*)*

VOICE OF TRUANT OFFICER: ...We will remember
this day...the sun will never seem so bright again....
Our days will grow dimmer and dimmer, but in our
darkest moment...we will remember this....

MACMANN: Yes...the lake...yes...there *was* a place...
where for the briefest moment...a glimpse.... Where was
that lake? Could I find it again if I tried? I don't know.
Have I ever seen anything to completion? No. But this
time I will. Yes, I have to go back and find that lake.
And when I find it...and when I find it...I will drown
myself in it....

(Music and lights out on all but GOAT*)*

END OF ACT ONE

ACT TWO

(We hear a jumbled montage, beginning gently and becoming more nightmarish, of various old songs on top of each other, as well as sound effects of tramcars, slammed doors, shouts, bleating, wind and whatnot. As sounds begin to fade, lights up on GOAT singing desperately)

GOAT: ...la la...la...la la... *(Pause)* Lest you think it's lessening...not a chance. Still ever-blossoming. The pain. Help me, brain. Help me manage it. If I knew the source of it, that would be a start. But I've not a clue. So scenes...of even greater beauty, the only hope now.

(We hear lovely music, and, concurrently, see a dim glow floating very slowly down to the stage)

GOAT: And what is that now? In inner world. That light. A falling star? Possibly. It's a puzzler though, for I have it on good authority that a bird ejected that light, from its bottom. Oh hello then. We know now. It's glowworm! Our Mister Fellow! Eaten by crow and half-digested, ejected out again, and now floating down...floating...lovely...I think he is a falling star of sorts. And now he's resting. Enduring. How does he do it? Yield up your secrets O glowworm! *(Pause)* I'm listening. *(Pause)* Well, you let me know when you're ready. *(Pause)* Thinks. I wonder if anyone else saw that last scene of great beauty, of glowworm descending. They could have seen it from a cottage window, perhaps. Marveaux, perhaps.

(Lights up on MARVEAUX *at window. Song on gramophone playing.* PHILOMEL, *now with legs, seated looking through phonographs.* MARVEAUX *gasps—)*

MARVEAUX: Will Wonders never cease!

PHILOMEL: What is it!? Do you see him!?

MARVEAUX: What? Who? Oh... No. It was just a glowworm—

PHILOMEL: Look, I'm beginning to lose my patience. I thought you said you knew where Halliwell was.

MARVEAUX: I do!

PHILOMEL: Then what, Marveaux Marveaux, are we doing here in this hovel?

MARVEAUX: But this isn't a hovel, dearest dear!

PHILOMEL: Then what do you call it?

MARVEAUX: Home sweet home!

PHILOMEL: I see.

MARVEAUX: It's stitched on that pillow.

PHILOMEL: Yes, I see.

MARVEAUX: For easy reference.

PHILOMEL: Noted. And what do you call sitting about for weeks on end without a sign of Halliwell?

MARVEAUX: I call it...

PHILOMEL: Yes?

MARVEAUX: I call it....

PHILOMEL: You don't know where he is. I'm leaving.

MARVEAUX: No, no! Wait!

PHILOMEL: Yes?

MARVEAUX: I call it...

PHILOMEL: You've wasted my time.

MARVEAUX: You can't call it all wasted!

PHILOMEL: Name one moment that wasn't utter misery.

MARVEAUX: You enjoyed the tour of the Century Biscuit Works.

PHILOMEL: It's true. Watching the Allis-Chalmers induction motors driving dough mixers was very edifying, and I've sent away for their Bulletin. But other than that, we've hardly gone outside! How are we going to find him if we stay in every day listening to phonographs and drinking warm mugs of tea?!

MARVEAUX: But what could be lovelier! I mean, must we look for him at all? You said once that you loved me.

PHILOMEL: I said it only because I wanted to see you drown.

MARVEAUX: Oh. *(Pause)* And...do you still want to see me drown?

PHILOMEL: Oh No, of course not. I love you.

MARVEAUX: You love me? O Joy and Happiness are Mine! *(Sighs with weight of great secret)* Well the truth is...there's two problems...regarding Halliwell. Firstly, if I risk wandering about the city looking for him— the military authorities will surely find me! I'm still wanted for desertion you know.

PHILOMEL: Yes I know.

MARVEAUX: And they'll shoot me.

PHILOMEL: Don't I know it.

MARVEAUX: So that's one problem.

PHILOMEL: And the other problem?

MARVEAUX: The other problem...the other problem...
(He suddenly begins trembling with tears and doubles over.)...oh god....

PHILOMEL: What? What is it?

MARVEAUX: *(Through streams of tears, shivering)* I...I can't
go on living this lie...the other problem...is that I did
something horrible...my childhood friend...I...killed him.

PHILOMEL: You what?

MARVEAUX: I was hoping you'd forget about him....
I was hoping I'd forget about him....but that bewildered
horrified face staring up at me in the woods, no, that
single image is seared into my soul for the rest of my
days...

PHILOMEL: ...I see.... *(Assessing emotional state)*
Interesting...I thought Halliwell might have been
different.

MARVEAUX: *(Through tears)* Perhaps you didn't care for
him after all!

PHILOMEL: Perhaps not.

MARVEAUX: So is there hope, is there hope for us?

(Just then, there is a knock on the door)

MARVEAUX: Who could that be?

*(MARVEAUX opens the door, and we see HALLIWELL,
nearly unrecognizable from his injuries and his expression
of pure bloody vengeance)*

HALLIWELL: ...The bogs...the wolves...

PHILOMEL: Halliwell!

MARVEAUX: Halliwell?! My friend! How...overjoyed
I am to see you!

HALLIWELL: *(Still with vengeance in eye)* And I you
Marveaux. And I you. Ah Phyllis, how's tricks.

PHILOMEL: I was told you were dead.

HALLIWELL: Disappointed?

PHILOMEL: Absolutely.

HALLIWELL: Disappointed that I was dead,
or disappointed that I'm still alive?

PHILOMEL: Wouldn't you like to know.

HALLIWELL: What a great tiresome flirt you are.

PHILOMEL: That's a cruel thing to say.

HALLIWELL: I suppose I need to be taught some
manners.

PHILOMEL: Yes you do.

HALLIWELL: And you'll do the teaching? A caning if
I'm bad, a kiss if I'm good?

PHILOMEL: And if you're *very* good—

HALLIWELL: I don't have time for this now. Marveaux—

MARVEAUX: Yes, my friend, dear friend.

HALLIWELL: We have some unfinished business.

MARVEAUX: If you think you're going to take me back
to the regiment—

HALLIWELL: That's not my plan at all.

MARVEAUX: No? Oh thank god!

HALLIWELL: No, I'm simply going to kill you. Right
here. Right now.

MARVEAUX: No! Wait! You can't! We're childhood
friends!

HALLIWELL: Hah!

MARVEAUX: What are you going to do?!

HALLIWELL: Strangle the life out of you.

PHILOMEL: Ooh this should be a pleasure to watch.

HALLIWELL: No no Fishy, this isn't some floor show. Come on, Marveaux.

MARVEAUX: Where are you taking me?

HALLIWELL: Your last moments are going to be spent in the privy.

MARVEAUX: *(Crying piteously, screaming)* No! No! Somebody Help! Philomel! Help me! For god's sake, Halliwell, please! Don't kill me!

(MARVEAUX *struggles mightily but* HALLIWELL *drags him offstage. The privy door slams. Silence.* PHILOMEL *selects a phonograph.)*

PHILOMEL: *(Reading)* "What Does it Matter", Columbia Records. *(She places the needle on the record, approving—)* It is of superior design. The soundbox. "Warm mugs of tea listening to phonographs." There *is* something to it. Hearthfire. A cozy room. *(Looking out window)* Pity about that goat outside. He looks hungry and sad. Maybe I should I invite him in!

(She heads to front door, when suddenly we hear the privy door open offstage.)

PHILOMEL: That was the door to the privy. He's done it. Come closer so I can congratulate you properly!

(MARVEAUX *enters, blood-stained and wild-eyed.)*

MARVEAUX: ...good god...the horror...

PHILOMEL: Marveaux!? How is it possible?!

MARVEAUX: I don't know...but he's dead...that bewildered horrified face staring up at me in the privy, no, that single image is seared into my soul for the rest of my days...

PHILOMEL: *(Terribly distressed, heads toward privy)* Halliwell!

MARVEAUX: *(Blocking her way)* No, don't go in.

PHILOMEL: *(Kissing* MARVEAUX *on face, on head, in desperate state)* You have to save him. You have to go get help.

MARVEAUX: But he's—

PHILOMEL: Surely there's still a chance. You'll never forgive yourself if you don't try.

MARVEAUX: But what if I'm captured?

PHILOMEL: You'll risk it for him.

MARVEAUX: But if he's dead—

PHILOMEL: Then risk it for me. I love you, I love you Marveaux. I will always wait for you. Be it months, be it years...but please....

MARVEAUX: ...O Fate...yes I'll go...just...give me something of yours...to remind me of you...a lock of hair...a perfumed handkerchief monogrammed with your initials—

PHILOMEL: Take this.

MARVEAUX: A used tram ticket. *(He clutches it to his breast, near tears.)* More precious still. For this pitiable scrap of paper has now bravely taken on a responsibility unmatched by any tram ticket in the history of tram tickets—to bear silent testament to our love.... I will return, my love....

*(*MARVEAUX *exits.* HALLIWELL *crawls gasping into the room, soaked with blood.)*

HALLIWELL: ...where...in god's name...did he get... that straight razor....

PHILOMEL: ...well you're a sight aren't you...

HALLIWELL: *(Coughing blood)* ...safety razors...that's the thing nowadays...that man's privy's a disaster—not a single toiletry product's up to date...my intestines are coming out and my liver's in ribbons...

PHILOMEL: You've done it this time.

HALLIWELL: Great help you were, you fat flirt.

(PHILOMEL *cradles the dying* HALLIWELL *in her lap.*)

PHILOMEL: I've never seen such a lousy fighter.

HALLIWELL: ...that's right, keep those cooing phrases coming....

PHILOMEL: I don't think I like your moustache.

HALLIWELL: Well then I'm definitely keeping it. Your legs could do with a shave.

PHILOMEL: That's the first thing you've said about my legs. Aren't you impressed?

HALLIWELL: I liked your flippers better.

PHILOMEL: They weren't flippers.

HALLIWELL: Hooves.

PHILOMEL: Hooves!

HALLIWELL: Wings, tentacles, whatever. What a sap he was to fall for you. It's just a lie you know. Love.

PHILOMEL: I know.

HALLIWELL: I know you know.

PHILOMEL: How can they put their trust in it?

HALLIWELL: They're all saps.

PHILOMEL: And their faith.

HALLIWELL: Saps.

PHILOMEL: They'll even pledge their lives to each other.

HALLIWELL: Great airedale terriers, all of them.

PHILOMEL: And yet...

HALLIWELL: What.

PHILOMEL: You want a last laugh?

HALLIWELL: Why not.

PHILOMEL: All right. Halliwell...

HALLIWELL: Phyllis.

PHILOMEL: I think I love you.

HALLIWELL: What?

PHILOMEL: I love you.

HALLIWELL: *(Laughing and it hurts)* ...oh it hurts...
there's the only thing I like about you, Phyllis...
you don't go in for that dried flower and doily chat.

PHILOMEL: You have me all wrong.

HALLIWELL: Oh yes?

PHILOMEL: I too have yearnings for domestic bliss.

HALLIWELL: Oh stop...you're killing me...I can just see
you at your needlepoint.

PHILOMEL: And why not?

HALLIWELL: What a wife you'd be!

PHILOMEL: And you'd be the worst husband in history.

HALLIWELL: Now wait a minute. You haven't seen me
poach a fish.

PHILOMEL: You can't poach a fish.

HALLIWELL: I can! I learned it from my father....
Dear old Fa...I wonder where he's at...haven't seen
him for years...he gets confused now...he's older....
(His pain intensifies.) I'm dying...what am I doing here—

PHILOMEL: You came seeking Marveaux—

HALLIWELL: No...I mean earth...what am I doing... what is any of us doing here... I'm going to take my trousers off—

PHILOMEL: What are you doing—stay still—

HALLIWELL: Shoes first...ouch... There... And now my trousers—

PHILOMEL: No. Stop moving—

HALLIWELL: I'm taking them off! ...Good...now lay them out so I can see them—

PHILOMEL: Sssh... Just think of breathing.

HALLIWELL: There's no reason to breathe...no reason to live..the only thing I ever loved was that pair of trousers—

PHILOMEL: I've seen nicer.

GOAT: Like hell you have. Well Phyllis, another notch in your little Siren book. You giant tart.

PHILOMEL: Gasbag.

HALLIWELL: Grandmother's knickers.

PHILOMEL: Old mule.

HALLIWELL: To hell with it... *(Now delirious)* Scraps of rubbish, that's all it was, half a caption from a soiled periodical and once a day the slop in the trough, if they even remembered...Except once..I thought I had soared through the heavens...starfield...but no...It was only a dream...*(He nearly dies; then, breathing heavily, with wide wild eyes, glowing with beatitude—)* ...but then...after he awoke, he found a speck of stardust in his hand...it was true...he had touched a star...

(HALLIWELL *dies.*)

PHILOMEL: ...Dead...he's dead....*(Lying)* and his death does not affect me...he meant nothing to me....

(HALLIWELL *revives with a groan.*)

HALLIWELL: ...you know what...

PHILOMEL: *(Terribly happy)* Halliwell, you're alive!

HALLIWELL: I thought of something to live for.

PHILOMEL: What.

HALLIWELL: Oh god.

PHILOMEL: What.

HALLIWELL: Don't make me say it.

PHILOMEL: Say what? *(Pause)*

HALLIWELL: Marry me.

PHILOMEL: *(Confident, without moment's hesitation)* I will.

HALLIWELL: You will?

PHILOMEL: I will marry you. Absolutely I will marry you!

(Music surges to coda, and lights out on all but GOAT.*)*

GOAT: Lovely! Lovely! That did the trick. Even now, still, the pain's remaining at bay. Though less at bay now. And less so now. And much less now. And definitely not now. And now it's worse. And now— *(He cries, and with desperation through pain—)* Quick, what was it Halliwell said, he has a father, I didn't know that, but it makes sense, he said his father's confused, and I'm confused, then that's what I am then, I'm somebody's father!

PHILOMEL: So we're really getting married!

HALLIWELL: If only father could see it!

PHILOMEL: Tell me more about your father.

HALLIWELL: Oh what's there to say. He wakes up every morning, dresses, dottle-trots down to the pub where he sings the old songs. He isn't much, but he's my dad.

Oh, and he was the second man to swim the English channel.

PHILOMEL: Well that is something. Then your father must be T W Burgess.

HALLIWELL: The very man.

PHILOMEL: My!

HALLIWELL: He's older now of course.

PHILOMEL: Relate to me an episode from his life. An episode of great loveliness.

HALLIWELL: The elder Halliwell, T W Burgess, sleeping. Brief respite from terrible aches of age. And decay of mind. Dreamless rest. Then suddenly, cells in his head misfire, causing, in his brain, pain. The most unspeakable pain in the history of man.

(Lights up on ELDER HALLIWELL *waking up with a yell, played by same actor as* GOAT)

ELDER HALLIWELL: I'm up! It hurts! I'm up! It hurts! *(Pain subsides)* Good. Now then. Hello bluebird. It's nice to be somebody's father, isn't it. And a channel swimmer to boot. Well, time to get up fellow. On with your clothes. Button the vest. Straighten the tie. Ready then? Good. Hold on. Trousers! Mustn't forget those. Funny. Where's my trousers. Check under the bed. No, not under bed. Thinks. My trousers. Thinks. I used to be a channel swimmer. Thinks. Holy Saint Martin! The only plausible explanation is that I left my trousers at the lake of my youth where I used to swim, for training, fifty years ago! Oh what to do! Must be very far away that lake. In space. In time. Could I find it if I tried? Do I have a choice? Nay! I'll go. I'll find the lake and trousers of my youth, and when I find them, and when I find them...I'll put them on. A clanking goat bell round my neck so I can't get lost and I'm off.

HALLIWELL: And off he goes.

(ELDER HALLIWELL, *trouserless and with goat bell tied with twine around his neck wanders off.*)

PHILOMEL: Mind you, another explanation, Halliwell, is that his trousers are simply hanging in his closet.

HALLIWELL: Yes.

PHILOMEL: And not at the lake of his youth at all.

HALLIWELL: But it's too late. He's on his way.

ELDER HALLIWELL: I'm on my way! La la la la La— Hang on. Did I leave the gas on? Can't remember. Better head back, always good to check. Now then, where's my flat. To the left. No. To the right. Two lefts. Help. Turn back again. One left, two rights. No. Help! One left. Help! I'm lost! Help! Help! ...Help! ...Help!...

(*Lights fade on* ELDER HALLIWELL, *we hear a slow military drumroll which continues throughout the following scene, and lights up on* MARVEAUX, *who has just been pushed to the ground near a wall. He has his hands tied behind his back. It is snowing.* MACMANN *is already standing against the wall, with his hands tied behind his back.*)

OFFSTAGE SOLDIER: Stand up!

(MARVEAUX *struggles to his feet with amazing difficulty thanks to having no hands for support, he turns on stomach, and back again, feet sliding against ground, etc.*)

OFFSTAGE SOLDIER: Stand up!

(*More amazing struggling.* MARVEAUX *finally manages to stand.*)

OFFSTAGE SOLDIER: Against the wall!

MARVEAUX: So this is it, Marveaux. The end of the line. A firing squad, a rain of bullets, death, death!

MACMANN: And yet...there's snow.... See how gently it falls.

MARVEAUX: Yes, how wondrous that soon it will cover all in a blanket of transcendent whiteness.

MACMANN: True, including our corpses.

MARVEAUX: Our corpses..God no, not our corpses! Help!

MACMANN: It's too late.

MARVEAUX: Are you here as well for desertion of ranks?

MACMANN: To tell you the truth, I have no idea what I'm doing here. My name is Macmann.

MARVEAUX: Marveaux.

OFFSTAGE SOLDIER: Ready! Aim!

MACMANN: Well it was grand talking with you Marveaux.

MARVEAUX: It was nice meeting you too, Macmann.

MACMANN: I have to tell you, this isn't how I wanted to die at all.

MARVEAUX: I understand. But I tell you what. This isn't *when* I wanted to die. *When.* The word in the sentence being.. "when."

MACMANN: Such plans I had...I was going to drown myself in the lake of my youth.

MARVEAUX: Why would you want to do that.

MACMANN: Tis a long story.

MARVEAUX: I love long stories.

MACMANN: Yes, but...

OFFSTAGE SOLDIER: Aim!

MARVEAUX: *(Quickly, in desperation)* Then just tell me this. What was the point to any of this?

MACMANN: It's a puzzler.

MARVEAUX: Did you ever have a dream of how things could be? A single moment even, of o'erwhelming beauty? For me, it was the promise of living my life with a woman named Philomel. As lovely as any wrapper on any cake of soap in the world.

MACMANN: She sounds indeed lovely. As for me— my dream was of creating a self-filling toilet.

MARVEAUX: There are tears in my eyes at the hearing of it.

MACMANN: A commode with a chamber that fills again with water after every flush, and stops filling automatically, without human intervention.

MARVEAUX: What happened?

MARVEAUX: I couldn't do it. All great inventions hinge on a principle of nature—

MARVEAUX: For instance?

MACMANN: Gravity—things fall down if you don't hold them up.

MARVEAUX: Trousers for instance.

MACMANN: Yes, or picture frames.

MARVEAUX: And hence—

MACMANN: Elastic suspenders and the wall bracket.

MARVEAUX: Two priceless enduring gifts to humanity.

MACMANN: There's a principle of nature that I can't remember, or that I never knew, and without it, all my struggling was in vain...and now—

OFFSTAGE SOLDIER: Aim!

MARVEAUX: And now...

OFFSTAGE SOLDIER: Fire!

(We hear the report of a dozen rifles. MACMANN *and* MARVEAUX *are thrown back to the wall and they slump to the ground, dead. Lights out on all but* GOAT.*)*

GOAT: I wonder. It's well-known that final thoughts are the most beautiful thoughts. What lovely thoughts then, must have been contained in the brains of Macmann and Marveaux, just as the bullets approached them at those remarkable speeds. That would make for a bit of distracting exquisiteness.

(Lights up on MACMANN *and* MARVEAUX *as we saw them moments earlier)*

MACMANN: —that I can't remember, or that I never knew, and without it, all my struggling was in vain....and now—

OFFSTAGE SOLDIER: Aim!

MARVEAUX: And now...

OFFSTAGE SOLDIER: Fire!

(We hear the report of a dozen rifles. We then hear the amplified heartbeat of MARVEAUX *and* MACMANN *while—)*

MACMANN: Dear Mother, I shall see you soon! Or no, I shall see only black and nothing. How strange that now my thoughts turn from Mother to Molly, and now from Molly to Kathleen, O sweet young Kathleen! You were the one for me, I know that now! Are you thinking of me tonight? Do you ever regret cutting me loose that dark day so many years ago?

(Lights up on KATHLEEN*)*

KATHLEEN: I should never have cut Macmann loose that terrible day. I was young, how was I to know, that he was the one? Perhaps I should give him a call. Yes. And we'll reunite, and everything in life will be right again! *(She picks up phone.)* Hello, operator, please connect me with Woodbine 8-3000, and hurry....yes, just tell him it's Kathleen...what?...It's disconnected?...

(Lights down on KATHLEEN, *lights up full on* MACMANN *and* MARVEAUX, *heartbeat still heard)*

MACMANN: Kathleen O Kathleen!

MARVEAUX: Philomel! My last thoughts and I find my brain flapping like a great hawk, or white snowy owl, to you. You pledged your love as I left you, and you gave me your....wait a minute...oh god! what did I do with that tram ticket....I had it when I left, didn't I... Yes, I put it in my breast pocket, and took it out again at Sandymount, no, that jacket didn't have a breast pocket, or was I even wearing a jacket, no, I changed jackets in Dalkey, that's what it was, in that shop...wait a minute, that man didn't give me the right change for the jacket did he—it was two and seven and fourpence and I gave him five, so I should have gotten three and three back, no, two and seven, or no, two and three, and six pence, but if he gave me twelve shillings and eight pence, wait, that can't be right, two and three, subtracted from seven, that's six and four, minus the eight pence....

(And overlapping with last part of above—)

MACMANN: Kathleen O Kathleen, those days of yore...you sat on the handlebars of my Raleigh Rustless and down the hills we sped, wind through your hair...your grin, such freedom...I'm a blink from death and I hear in my mind's ear the ring of that bicycle bell...

KATHLEEN: I bought it for you—remember?

MACMANN: You've a heart as large as the sea! ...Twas a genuine Lucas-challis that bell!

KATHLEEN: Very rigidly constructed.

MACMANN: Loud and effective was the ring. I saw it in the catalogue for two and nine. But then you said—

KATHLEEN: I got a better bargain.

MACMANN: Better than two and nine? O I kissed your sweet face—

KATHLEEN: And you whispered in my ear—

MACMANN: Do you think then you could be getting a pump for my tyres? The Bluemel "Unicorn" is the best. I could get it for six and two but I can't afford six and two, but if you could get it for five and eight, I could chip in two and three, which would leave three and nine—

MARVEAUX: change for the jacket was two and seven, or no, two and three, and six pence, but wait, two and three subtracted from seven, that's six and four minus the eight...	MACMANN: no, three and six, wait, eight shillings for the pump and if two and three plus three and six, no, I mean four, carry the two...

(MACMANN *and* MARVEAUX *pursue their computations simultaneously, and then, the heartbeats stop, they're chests both shudder, they're thrown back against the wall, and they slump to the ground, dead. Lights out on all but* GOAT.)

GOAT: The brain is very fast isn't it. To think all those thoughts. It's no wonder then that so much pain of mine can be packed into a single millysecond...and every millysecond thereafter.

(*Lights up on* MACMANN *and* MARVEAUX, *standing as they were twice previous*)

MACMANN: —that I can't remember, or that I never knew, and without it, all my struggling was in vain...and now—

OFFSTAGE SOLDIER: Aim!

MARVEAUX: And now...

OFFSTAGE SOLDIER: Fire!

(We hear the report of a dozen rifles. MACMANN and MARVEAUX are thrown back to the wall and they slump to the ground, dead. Lights out on all but GOAT.)

GOAT: Aye, the brain's fast alright. Now then... lovely things...please...lovely things...

(Lights up on PHILOMEL and HALLIWELL in MARVEAUX's cottage. PHILOMEL in chair reading through classifieds with pencil. HALLIWELL whistling as he jauntily packs a suitcase)

GOAT: ...lovely...lovely—

PHILOMEL: Puppies!

HALLIWELL: Certainly not. Put that paper down. *(Resumes packing)* Three white shirts, trousers—

PHILOMEL: But why not?

HALLIWELL: Why not what.

PHILOMEL: Puppies! Oh please...please...it would be so nice—

HALLIWELL: No. Where are my ties?

PHILOMEL: But it makes a home so much homier.

HALLIWELL: So does a porcelain duck. Honey, where are my ties?

PHILOMEL: But I've never had a puppy.

HALLIWELL: You were too busy drowning people.

PHILOMEL: *(Circling ad)* Ooh look here's a setter on sale, and it's just up the street—

HALLIWELL: Nothing doing—I see right through your little scheme.

PHILOMEL: What scheme?

HALLIWELL: Gals get engaged and first thing off the bat it's puppies.

PHILOMEL: Because they're nice.

HALLIWELL: No, because they do in a man's hard-won convictions.

PHILOMEL: I'm sure I don't know what you're talking about.

HALLIWELL: Oh don't you Sally Siren. You know what'll happen if I get a puppy. I'll be up all hours housetraining it, worrying myself sick when it gets a cough, thrilled to the gills with having a little nipper romping about, and Good God woman, before I blink, I'm the father of ten screaming children wiping their noses on everything I own, and then I'm *stuck but good.*

PHILOMEL: Oh.

HALLIWELL: So there.

PHILOMEL: Darling.

HALLIWELL: What.

PHILOMEL: I've never heard anything more ridiculous. Don't you trust me?

HALLIWELL: Trust you? Honey, for all I know you still want me dead.

PHILOMEL: Not for all the tea in China!

HALLIWELL: Yeah, well it's still just good policy for a husband-to-be.

PHILOMEL: But—

HALLIWELL: No puppies. *(He kisses her.)* Now then. I'll be back at eight—

PHILOMEL: Where are you going?

HALLIWELL: To the club.

PHILOMEL: Not again!

HALLIWELL: I want to get in a swim before my business trip.

PHILOMEL: Oh can't you just stay in tonight? I won't see you for three whole days when you leave tomorrow.

HALLIWELL: But I have to get a shave.

PHILOMEL: Shave here.

HALLIWELL: Shave here? But they do a much better job at the—

PHILOMEL: *(Disappearing into the privy)* I'll shave you.

HALLIWELL: You? Hey, waitaminute—

PHILOMEL: *(Returning with straight razor, brush, and cream)* Watch, I'll show you, and then you'll never have to go to the club again—

HALLIWELL: Hold on—

PHILOMEL: *(Lathering him up)* Hold still—

HALLIWELL: I won't let you shave me—

PHILOMEL: Relax...

HALLIWELL: But—

PHILOMEL: Just relax, you'll enjoy it.

HALLIWELL: Fine.

PHILOMEL: Now then...we'll start with the neck, close your eyes...you won't feel a thing...

(PHILOMEL, *standing behind a seated* HALLIWELL, *has razor poised at his neck, when* HALLIWELL *leaps up, afright)*

PHILOMEL: What is it.

HALLIWELL: *(Breathing heavily)* I can't.

PHILOMEL: ...What... You don't trust me do you....

HALLIWELL: No.

PHILOMEL: I don't want you dead.

HALLIWELL: Sure you don't.

PHILOMEL: How are we going to get married if—

HALLIWELL: I don't know.

PHILOMEL: Listen to me—

HALLIWELL: How am I supposed to trust you when I know what you've been.

PHILOMEL: It's just a leap of faith.

HALLIWELL: Just!

PHILOMEL: Listen to me—

HALLIWELL: No—

PHILOMEL: We're done for if you don't come and sit down right now. Look at me...and entrust to me your fate....

HALLIWELL: Are you so sure you're not what you were?

PHILOMEL: I think so.

HALLIWELL: I have no proof. Nothing to rely on at all.

PHILOMEL: We are constructing a life together—is that not wondrous enough for you? Imagine what joys still lay ahead!

(Pause, then finally—)

HALLIWELL: *(To self)* ...it's only life...it's only life...

(And HALLIWELL, still lathered, sits down. PHILOMEL holds razor at neck. Her arm tenses, HALLIWELL grimaces, waiting for the worst. Pause. And then she shaves neck. As soon as HALLIWELL and PHILOMEL realize the threat to his life has passed, they look up at each other, and then kiss passionately. And then—)

PHILOMEL: So can we get the puppy?

(And as they kiss again still more passionately—)

GOAT: You can take apart this story piece by piece until it's a hundred pieces at your feet, but the beating heart of it you'll find here and here alone....A man, a woman who falls for a man who lets her shave him, and Swan's shaving soap, where a fraction of an inch, and I do mean a fraction, whips up into big, rich billowy waves of lather on your face. Available through Robbins and Myers, Limited, Dublin and all principal cities. *(Pause, then as* GOAT's *pain increases, he cries, grows vengeful, and spits out/frantically—)* Feed the guns with war bonds.... Feed the guns with war bonds.... Feed the guns with war bonds...and help to win the war—

MARVEAUX: Dear Philomel...my one, my love...

(We hear an approaching shell, and very loud explosion, the sound of gunfire, etc., and lights up on MARVEAUX *penning a letter, breathing heavily—clearly in pain— in a trench [W W I], shells exploding around him. He is wearing a large unflattering moustache.)*

MARVEAUX: ...I haven't much time...I don't how it's possible that I'm alive, I once was dead, I'm sure of it, but here I am alone in no-man's land and thinking of you...I was found as good as done for and conscripted by the enemy, I'm trapped, my leg torn to pieces by an exploding shell, it's going to have to come off, the pain lessens only when I think of your loveliness. I've grown a moustache just for you. I think you'll like it. I am holding in my hand your tram ticket, I thought I had lost it, what solace there is knowing you're remaining true to me...Keep the homefires burning, my darling, and I'll endeavor to get out of here in one piece, or rather, more than one, but less than three—

(Just then, there is an enormous explosion, and an OLD SOLDIER *[played by same actor as the* GOAT] *scurries into the trench.* MARVEAUX *grabs his rifle and points his bayonet*

at the OLD SOLDIER *as the* OLD SOLDIER *points his
bayonet at* MARVEAUX. *Pause. Then* MARVEAUX *screams,*
OLD SOLDIER *screams, and* MARVEAUX *rushes at the*
OLD SOLDIER, *plunging his bayonet into him. Preferably
we see more than a little blood.)*

OLD SOLDIER: I think you got me Jiffy....

MARVEAUX: Oh God...I'm sorry...I'm so sorry—

OLD SOLDIER: I'm not even the enemy.

MARVEAUX: You're not even the enemy.

OLD SOLDIER: I wouldn't have hurt you.

MARVEAUX: I hate this. I don't want to be alive...

OLD SOLDIER: Ah now, none of that...pack up your
troubles...chin chin...

MARVEAUX: Perhaps it's not so bad—

OLD SOLDIER: No no, I'm done for....

(MARVEAUX *cradles* OLD SOLDIER *in his lap as he is dying)*

MARVEAUX: Please...please don't die, I'll do anything
for you.

OLD SOLDIER: Anything? ...Well...you might sing me a
little song.

MARVEAUX: I can't sing.

OLD SOLDIER: Oh I don't mind that.... Do you know
(Sings) "A Bachelor Gay am I...though I'm wounded
by Cupid's dart...la la...la la...." I can't remember it...
I only heard songs through the window, you see, I was
outside, you see, attached to a post, by a tether...so long
ago it seems...rutting seasons came and went but even
that simple pleasure was denied me—

MARVEAUX: Ssh...you'll be fine....

OLD SOLDIER: I just need someone to cradle me...
that's all I ask...it's lonely in no man's land...Help!
Where are you! I can't see!

MARVEAUX: *(Beginning to sing softly)*
Don't....mind....the darkness...
Morning...will come....

MARVEAUX/OLD SOLDIER:
...shadows are bound to go by..
...and when they fly...
...rosy dawn will pierce the sky...and..."

(Just then, an enormous explosion rocks the stage, we hear screams, and lights go out. We then hear the OLD SOLDIER singing "La la la" to tune of "morning will come" and lights slowly up on MARVEAUX now in OLD SOLDIER's lap. MARVEAUX's left arm is missing)

MARVEAUX: What happened?

OLD SOLDIER: They got you but good, the dirty Hun—

MARVEAUX: Are you still dying?

OLD SOLDIER: Of course I'm still dying. But now you're giving me some company in that department.

MARVEAUX: ...Hey! ...Hey! Where's my arm!

OLD SOLDIER: Don't fret it, I managed a tourniquet on it.

MARVEAUX: *(Screaming)* But what happened to it!

OLD SOLDIER: Shell took it right off, didn't it. Flew off like a little sparrow—

MARVEAUX: A little sparrow! That's my arm you're talking about! Oh god!

OLD SOLDIER: You can see it way over there now, where that stray dog is sniffing.

MARVEAUX: *(Calling out to dog)* Hey! Get away from that!

OLD SOLDIER: Where are you going!

MARVEAUX: I have to retrieve it—it's clutching a very special scrap of paper—

OLD SOLDIER: *(Holding him back)* Go out there and it's your head'll be flying off next.

MARVEAUX: I don't care.... *(Seeing dog)* No! The cursed dog's running off with my arm! Hey! Come back here! *(As a serious dog owner)* Come. No, bad dog. *(Firmly)* Come. Come!

OLD SOLDIER: And he's gone. Well, you gave it an effort.

MARVEAUX: *(Weeps)* I'll never see my arm again...What's a dog doing out there anyway.

OLD SOLDIER: Now now, you wouldn't believe some of the heroism of dogs in this war. Terriers in particular. Scampering cross no-man's land, delivering messages of national import—

MARVEAUX: You're right. You don't have to be a human being to have worth.

OLD SOLDIER: Even though the dog is just an animal, it is noble and good and true.

MARVEAUX: Would that I were a dog.

OLD SOLDIER: Perhaps I *am* a dog, and not a soldier. That would make sense.

MARVEAUX: Yes, that would make sense.

OLD SOLDIER: Tethered outside cottage by day, but at night, inside, me, on hearth rug, warm, happy dreams of chasing rabbits. And committing all sorts of heroic deeds in times of national emergency.

(We hear MACMANN.)

OLD SOLDIER: Rescuing good men like Macmann.

(Lights up on the now-blind MACMANN screaming on a hospital cot, entire head and eyes covered in bandages.

*A W W I nurse [*KATHLEEN*] comes to assist him.*
Next to MACMANN's *bed is the* GOAT.)

MACMANN: God in Heaven, I cannot see!

KATHLEEN: Sssh. Rest now. I'll adjust your bandages—

MACMANN: Where am I?

KATHLEEN: Hospital. Two miles from the front.

MACMANN: How did I get here?

KATHLEEN: You were very lucky. *(Indicating* GOAT*)*
You were saved by this dog. He risked his own life to
save yours.

MACMANN: I can't see him. Tell me... Is he a fox terrier?

KATHLEEN: ...I don't know.... *(She begins to weep.)*

MACMANN: Or perhaps an old english sheep dog?

KATHLEEN: He might be....

MACMANN: Well I tell you this—I'll take him with me.
I'll adopt him, and—what is it... Are you crying?

KATHLEEN: ...the suffering I've seen here..and yet every
man and dog enduring it all without complaint—

GOAT: Imagine that—tears for a dog... And he said he'd
adopt me.... Is there anything man can't extend his
endless compassion to?

KATHLEEN: *(Through tears)* Let me adjust your blankets.
And now a blanket for the dog.

GOAT: Blankets are nice. On everything. Lovely
blankets. "On his cold beef, he ran a blanket of mustard
across." I've seen that before.

(We hear birdsong, the bleat of distant sheep, the low of cows,
and lights up on HALLIWELL, *whistling, straddling a bicycle,*
and holding a sandwich in one hand, a knife in the other)

GOAT: Oh yes, we'll divert from one scene of beauty for yet another—

HALLIWELL: A spring breeze, the song of the bluebird—

GOAT: And a sandwich.

HALLIWELL: *(Pleased with life)* No more the motor car, no, nor the tramcar for me. Every business trip should be from now on, taken on bicycle. And here's the caption—

(We hear achingly beautiful music.)

GOAT: "On his cold beef, he ran a blanket of mustard across. He was glad that in his sack, he had remembered...the mustard.

HALLIWELL: Colmans mustard.

GOAT: And here's the most exciting part of all.

HALLIWELL: *(Slowly, radiating inner spiritual peace—)* There are two more sandwiches in my sack.

GOAT: The end.

MACMANN: Well I tell you this—I'll take him with me. I'll adopt him, and—what is it... Are you crying?...

KATHLEEN: ...the suffering I've seen here..and yet every man and dog and cricket player enduring it all without complaint—

MACMANN: You mustn't take it to heart—

KATHLEEN: No...no I *must* take it to heart...the heart is like an inverted type recording gauge, it is creation's electrical indicating meter by which we may read and decipher the world...Jettison the heart and you're left with the dark abysm of incomprehension. I know of what I speak, because I sent away the love of my life long ago.

MACMANN: My deep condolences.

KATHLEEN: Thank you.

MACMANN: Hang on... Did you say "man and dog and *cricket player*?

KATHLEEN: Oh yes, there are many cricket players in this ward. Mister A C MacLaren of Lancashire is two beds down, lung collapsed by poison gas, T Hayward—

MACMANN: —of Surrey!

KATHLEEN: Third degree burns.

MACMANN: G.L. Jessop?

KATHLEEN: Having an arm amputated as we speak. In fact, nearly the entire roster of cricketers represented by the 1912 Wills Cigarettes Series—

MACMANN: I know that series!

KATHLEEN: Isn't it wizard?!

MACMANN: Aye, and better still—it's bright clouds and a leap in the heart...I knew a girl once...long ago... next to my mother, she was the entire world to me... and she had the whole series.

KATHLEEN: *I* had the whole series...

MACMANN: Your voice—it sounds so familiar.

KATHLEEN: I knew a boy who wanted to be an inventor—

MACMANN: She sat on the handlebars of my Raleigh Rustless and down the hills we sped—

KATHLEEN: Macmann—

MACMANN: Kathleen—

KATHLEEN: My love.

MACMANN: Marry me.

KATHLEEN: I will.

MACMANN: You will?

KATHLEEN: Yes...yes...I will!

MACMANN: Then get these blankets off of me...
We're going home!

(Beautiful music as MACMANN *and* KATHLEEN *leave,
leaving* GOAT *alone on stage.)*

GOAT: *(Calling out)* Hey, and what about the dog?
You were going to adopt the dog! *(Beat)* Very
interesting. They abandon the dog. The end. *(Bitterly)*
Blankets. Nothing's lovely about blankets. Nothing's
lovely about loveliness. On his cold beef, he ran a
blanket of mustard across. Could it be that that
loveliness could be...his undoing...

(We hear HALLIWELL *whistling offstage, then see him
whistling as he glides slowly across stage on bicycle.*

GOAT: Yes. It could.

HALLIWELL: *(Stopping bicycle)* Did I just hear something
fall?

GOAT: On the ground, next to that lovely glowworm
that just got run over. Do you see it?

HALLIWELL: *(Checking trouser cuff)* My trouser clip!
It must have fallen off the cuff of my trousers.

GOAT: Will he go back and try to retrieve it?

HALLIWELL: I would go back and look for it, but with
three sandwiches sloshing about in me, I think I'm
going to give it a miss. Trouser clips are generally
an unnecessary precaution and I still have time for a
steambath and a solid eight in Dreamland before the
business meeting tomorrow. So off we go.

(Lights down on all but GOAT.*)*

GOAT: Now then. It's been a lot of sweat and planning
involving trouser clips, but I think I've done it, I've

paved the way for the next scene of great beauty.
Are we ready? Now then. "Halliwell, what's happened
to Halliwell. And why has he stopped?"

(Lights up on HALLIWELL, *who is straddling bicycle with a
panicked look on his face, breathing heavily)*

HALLIWELL: Don't panic Sunny Jim, whatever you do.
Panic and you can say your goodbyes right now. Your
trousers are caught in the chain, yes. But with a little
finesse we'll be well out of it in no time, and with a
minimum of grief and permanent trouser stain.

*(*HALLIWELL *unstraddles bicycle, and attempts pulling
trousers out of the chain, but they're quite stuck. He pulls
harder. Then begins wrestling with bicycle, dragging himself
and cycle around the floor, ringing bell inadvertently, etc.
During which—)*

GOAT: That's a Bluemel "unicorn model" pump on the
frame there. Its celluloid barrel never develops cracks
or chips. That's the unicorn all over for you. Must be
lovely creatures beyond imagining. Unicorns. Pity
they're never seen—I bet they'd give you a lift just with
a glimpse. Oh look, night's descending.

*(We see night descend, the moon rises, we hear crickets chirp,
owls hoot, the sun rises, morning comes, Halliwell still
struggling with trousers, until at last—)*

HALLIWELL: *(Tears in eyes)* I can't believe it's come to
this...

(The music becomes achingly beautiful and melancholy.)

HALLIWELL: ...but have I a choice? *(And he takes off shoes
and pulls himself out of his trousers, leaving him in briefs.
He stands, considering the trousers and bicycle on ground.)*
...must I abandon you both? In time we say goodbye
to everything we ever knew, but how could I know it
would be so soon with you...

GOAT: How hard it must be! Poor Halliwell!

(*And as* HALLIWELL *walks slowly away, exiting, casting a glance back every now and then to scene of his despair*)

GOAT: Yes, you can take apart this story piece by piece but the beating heart of it you'll find here and here alone....Halliwell's trousers. And where's Philomel? Oh she's inside. Asleep.

(*Lights up on* PHILOMEL *asleep.*)

GOAT: Must be nice. One thing nicer. Rain. To sleep inside with rain outside. Well then, we'll have rain then. As a present. To her. (*And we hear rain*) Mind you, it's not such a nice present to any man caught outside in it. Not in that downpour. Halliwell for instance.

(*And as thunder rumbles, we see* HALLIWELL *in briefs, with rain sprinkling on him*)

HALLIWELL: Alright, let's think this out scientifically. I could run for shelter under that tree, but the more I move, the more wet the more of me will get. Right? So. Here's the plan. I'll stand absolutely still and wait for this little outburst to pass. After all, it's a truism of both pain and rain— "the stronger the episode, the sooner it ceases again." So. Here we go.

(HALLIWELL *stands still. Pause. More thunder, more rain. Pause. Looks at watch. More rain. Et cetera*)

HALLIWELL: It's going to stop. Any moment now. (*Long pause*) Any moment now. (*Long pause*) Okay, I'm getting a little wet. But I'm sticking to the plan. (*Pause*) Okay, I'm having a cigarette and thinking about revisions.

(HALLIWELL *takes cigarette from shirt pocket. Searches trousers pocket for matches. Realizes he's not wearing trousers. Now we see* KATHLEEN *with golf club sizing up a ball, blind* MACMANN *with golf bag and holding umbrella*

over KATHLEEN *as she prepares her shot.* HALLIWELL
crosses to her as she swings.)

KATHLEEN: Did you see where it went?

MACMANN: I believe it went straight and true O sweet
Kathleen, but tis only a guess, as it's dark, and it's
raining, and I'm completely blind.

HALLIWELL: Excuse me honey, but do you have a light?
I seem to have left my matches in my trousers.

KATHLEEN: Of course.

*(She strikes a match and he holds her hand to steady the
match)*

KATHLEEN: You didn't see where my ball went did you?

HALLIWELL: You sliced it.

KATHLEEN: No.

HALLIWELL: Believe it.

KATHLEEN: Damn.

HALLIWELL: You're bending your elbow when you
swing.

KATHLEEN: Thanks for the tip. I didn't know you were
watching me so closely.

HALLIWELL: It's hard not to.

KATHLEEN: *(Warningly)* Now look, I'm a happily
married woman.

HALLIWELL: I'm a happily married man.

KATHLEEN: So we're both happy.

HALLIWELL: Happy happy.

KATHLEEN: And yet—

HALLIWELL: Yes.

KATHLEEN: And it will be meaningless.

HALLIWELL: Utterly.

KATHLEEN: And marriage-threatening.

HALLIWELL: No doubt.

KATHLEEN: Is something Greater than us determining our lives?

HALLIWELL: Greater? I don't think so. One afternoon is all I can spare.

KATHLEEN: It's random and stupid.

HALLIWELL: Suddenly everything is.

KATHLEEN: If only we were pure.

HALLIWELL: Only two things are pure. The unicorn, and Swan's soap.

KATHLEEN: Have you ever seen a unicorn?

HALLIWELL: No, but I swear by Swan's.

KATHLEEN: So do I. The perfect cleanliness that results from its use makes it the soap most generally preferred for the bath.

HALLIWELL: And it's so pure, it floats.

KATHLEEN: I can't imagine such purity.

HALLIWELL: That's why we're already sinking.

KATHLEEN: Two o'clock, tomorrow.

HALLIWELL: Til then.

MACMANN: Darling, where are you? Can we go home now?

(*Lights up on* PHILOMEL *in cottage. A knock on the door.* PHILOMEL *opens it to find* MARVEAUX, *missing an arm and walking as if with wooden leg.*)

MARVEAUX: Philomel!

PHILOMEL: Marveaux?!

MARVEAUX: I made it! Heaven be praised!

PHILOMEL: I thought you were dead!

MARVEAUX: How could I die knowing you were here waiting for me! And now I'm home! I'm sure these last years of unwavering fidelity have taken their toll.

(Quite a long pause)

PHILOMEL: Well actually—

MARVEAUX: Oh if only you knew how happy you make me. Just standing there, just as you are, in our little cottage, the lingering homey smells of pipe tobacco and aftershave, as if I never left—

PHILOMEL: Yes, well actually—

MARVEAUX: Oh the old Victrola! How I missed it on the front, the front...what a...what a...chasm of terror...*(Breaks down weeping)* ...forgive me...

PHILOMEL: Certainly.

MARVEAUX: Forgive me...

PHILOMEL: Yes. Are you done...

MARVEAUX: Forgive me, it's just—

PHILOMEL: You needn't explain, and I have something to tell you—

MARVEAUX: And look! There above the hearth those carved words that in my memory I clutched to so tightly—

PHILOMEL: "Two lovebirds built this nest." Yes. However—

MARVEAUX: —and the old easy chair— *(He sits down.)* —it just shows you what luck and good fortune really mean—I could lose all my limbs, I could go blind and deaf and endure any sort of horrendous pain, so long as I had a love to share—what's this under the cushion.

(He pulls from under the chair cushion a pair of
HALLIWELL's *underpants. Confused—)* These aren't
my underpants. What does this mean?...Wait,
there's a name written on the band....(*Utterly
devastated*)..."Halliwell."

(At this moment, HALLIWELL *enters, carrying groceries,
looking hale and happy)*

HALLIWELL: Well I'm back from the grocers and what a
cucumber I bought, oh it's a beaut! *(Noticing)*
Marveaux! You?!

MARVEAUX: If you're thinking about killing me—

HALLIWELL: Killing you? My dear friend? I'm over the
moon to see you again. I felt sure you were dead.

MARVEAUX: *(Miserably)* And I, you.

HALLIWELL: Come closer so we can embrace fully.

MARVEAUX: Why aren't you dead?

HALLIWELL: Love, Marveaux, love. Perhaps one day
you too can experience the majesty of it. You're staying
for dinner aren't you?

MARVEAUX: No.

HALLIWELL: What?

MARVEAUX: I can't.

HALLIWELL: Oh you have to be crazy to pass up this.
I'm poaching a fish.

MARVEAUX: It hurts too much.

HALLIWELL: Red snapper! Honey, will you light the
oven?

MARVEAUX: How could you marry Halliwell?! How?!

PHILOMEL: He knows how to blow smoke rings.

HALLIWELL: Ain't she a treat.

MARVEAUX: So it's true?

HALLIWELL: Pipe, cigar, cigarette, it's true, but you knew that. Say chum, I got a couple Fatima Turkish Blend, they're a smooth smoke, they're mild, and yet they satisfy, what say you to a stroll in the garden and we can—

MARVEAUX: No, I have to go. My heart's about to explode.

HALLIWELL: You sound as if you're shell-shocked, man.

MARVEAUX: ...I am... *(He exits cottage.)*

GOAT: And above the hearth in his heart was carved this—

GOAT/MARVEAUX: "Alone I am, alone I'll always be... wondering where the weeping willow grows...."

(And as MARVEAUX *sings the below, or we hear a recording of the tune, the* GOAT *narrates—)*

MARVEAUX: *(Sings)*
Weeping willow true dear
There I'll seek for you dear
Dreams will never bring you back to me
Even in my fondest memories
You and I are strolling once again
Down in Weeping Willow Lane...

GOAT: Down the road he goes. Alone. If only he could speak to someone, the clouds even, or the Blackburn-Smith Enclosed Tank Switches at yonder Biscuit Works, but no...there is no one with whom to share his pain....

(And meanwhile, lights up on MACMANN *and* KATHLEEN*)*

MACMANN: Kathleen.

KATHLEEN: Yes dear.

MACMANN: Tis true that I'm blind.

KATHLEEN: I know darling, but it doesn't matter.

MACMANN: I am blind, and I dropped my cane and it rolled under the bed.

KATHLEEN: Did you find it? Do you need help?

MACMANN: No no. I found it. I also found this. *(He holds up a pair of underpants.)* I am blind, but I am not stupid. Or no, I am both blind and stupid. For this feels to me like a pair of men's undergarments. Am I right?

KATHLEEN: Yes.

MACMANN: They're not mine. Whose are they.

KATHLEEN: You don't know him.

MACMANN: What's his name.

KATHLEEN: You don't know him.

MACMANN: I'll be the judge of that.

KATHLEEN: But you've never heard of him, and it doesn't matter—

MACMANN: His name.

KATHLEEN: —and it didn't mean anything—

MACMANN: Who is the owner of these underpants!

KATHLEEN: Listen to me—

MACMANN: Give me the name!

KATHLEEN: Halliwell!

MACMANN: Halliwell! ...Who in Heaven is Halliwell?

KATHLEEN: You don't know him.

MACMANN: ...Oh...

KATHLEEN: ...And it doesn't matter...my darling...
it didn't mean anything—

MACMANN: Ah but there you're wrong, sweet sweet Kathleen.... Don't you know what faith is? Tis worthless scraps of paper that we agree to call the moon and sun until, miraculously, they *become* the moon and sun, and they remain so, until one of us loses faith, and suddenly they're scraps of paper again....Call it magic or call it Delusion, tis wonderful whatever it is.... But now... it's gone.

KATHLEEN: ...I'm so sorry....

MACMANN: We all make mistakes...we make nothing but...I called myself an inventor, but that was a delusion that had it's day.

KATHLEEN: Where are you going?

MACMANN: There was a moment, at the lake of my youth, when I was deluded and the world seemed to have meaning and beauty.... And now, bedad, I'm deluded yet again, and I *will* find it, I'll find that lake, and when I do....I shall drown myself in it if it kills me!

(*Lights up on* PHILOMEL *and* HALLIWELL)

HALLIWELL: Why are you looking at me like that.

PHILOMEL: Because I was so incredibly happy and now I realize I was just incredibly deluded.

HALLIWELL: What are you talking about.

PHILOMEL: I picked up the laundry from the shop and it came with a note of apology. "We are sorry, but we couldn't remove the lipstick from the shirt collar."

HALLIWELL: Don't be sad honey, I have other shirts.

PHILOMEL: It wasn't my shade of lipstick....

HALLIWELL: No?

PHILOMEL: There's also a pair of underpants missing.

HALLIWELL: Look, I don't know what you're suggesting but—

PHILOMEL: Yes you do...I was stupid...I of all people should have known better than to trust love.... Goodbye Halliwell.

HALLIWELL: Wait! *(She exits.)* ...And above the hearth was carved this... "Two lovebirds built this...this....

CLERK: ...passimeter booking equipment office."

(Lights up on MARVEAUX *and an old* CLERK, *perhaps played by same actor as* GOAT. *We hear the steady rhythm of the passimeter booking equipment [Suggesting a needle at the end of a phonograph])*

CLERK: To avoid congestion at the booking office windows of underground railway stations, passimeter booking equipment is utilized by the Passenger Transport Board.

MARVEAUX: Passimeter booking equipment. Yes.

CLERK: Aye. All this information, mind, can be found in the Wills Cigarette Series on Railway Equipment.

MARVEAUX: Good to know.

CLERK: Right then. Each ticket is dated and cancelled mechanically as the booking clerk removes it from the machine. Perfect job for war veterans like yourself.

MARVEAUX: I suppose. I just wanted a job underground, where I don't have to ever see the light of day again. So what's my job, specifically.

CLERK: Well in the passimeter booking office at stations where there are lifts, such as this one, the lift is controlled by the booking clerk.

MARVEAUX: So my new job, essentially—

CLERK: Is to operate the lift.

(Inside life, lever out of view of audience)

MARVEAUX: With this lever.

CLERK: Yes, it's very simple. Lift up. Lift down. Like so. You try it now.

MARVEAUX: Lift up. Lift down.

CLERK: No you did the exact opposite. Lift up. Lift down.

MARVEAUX: Lift up. Lift down.

CLERK: You just did the exact opposite again.

MARVEAUX: I can't do it.

CLERK: You can. Lift up. Lift down.

MARVEAUX: Right.

CLERK: No. Lift *up*, lift down.

MARVEAUX: I've nearly got it.

CLERK: Concentrate.

MARVEAUX: This is hard work.

CLERK: It's broken many a spirit.

MARVEAUX: Lift up, lift down. How's that?

CLERK: You got it completely wrong.

MARVEAUX: I hate this.

CLERK: This could take all week. Do you have anything to sustain you?

MARVEAUX: A sandwich. Just one. Lift up, lift down.

CLERK: That was horrible. And no, I mean do you perhaps have some great love who may bolster your courage in this time of trial? What? Is it something I said?

MARVEAUX: No, I'm fine. But to answer your question about that great love...the answer would be no. Lift up, lift down.

CLERK: No.

MARVEAUX: Lift up, lift down.

CLERK: Sweet Mary.

MARVEAUX: Lift up, lift down.

CLERK: We now skip ahead to many years later.

MARVEAUX: Lift up, lift down.

CLERK: Not quite.

MARVEAUX: Oh I understand now. Lift up, lift down.

CLERK: ...em...no.

MARVEAUX: I need a rest.

CLERK: We both do....Yes, come lean on my shoulder...gather your strength....

(*They lean on each other in embrace, and more sleepily—*)

MARVEAUX: Not quitting despite despair...

CLERK: ...just brief resting...

MARVEAUX: Plumbing depths for untapped reserves of fortitude...

CLERK: Dreaming...

MARVEAUX: I'm done with dreaming....

(*The rhythm of the booking equipment leads into beautiful music, and we hear* PHILOMEL *singing, distantly but getting closer, until the doors of the lift open, and she appears, singing* All Alone)

PHILOMEL: All alone, I was all alone And then I...found...you...

(*And as the music [*All Alone*] continues—*)

MARVEAUX: What are you doing here?

PHILOMEL: I had to come back to you. You're the only one I love....

MARVEAUX: I thought I'd never know how to smile again. And now...and now...I'm worried that I'll never stop...

(They kiss passionately, and lights out.)

GOAT: Lovely....The only problem for Marveaux being this—It was just a dream.

(And lights up abruptly, and MARVEAUX *is startled awake. He had fallen asleep in his chair. The clerk is gone.)*

MARVEAUX: It was just a dream? ...It was just a *dream*?! ...I can't stand it! Why do I wake up from *that*, instead of ever waking up from *this*, this dunghill...ah well... I suppose I'll go home for the night. *(He opens the door of the lift, steps in, and discovers—)* Halliwell!

HALLIWELL: Marveaux! What a small world it is!

MARVEAUX: It is we who are small. What are you doing here.

HALLIWELL: I just got off the train, I...I'm off to win back Philomel.

MARVEAUX: Win her back?

HALLIWELL: I lost her and it was all my fault, I was a heel, I cheated on her and took her for granted, and I sat around for a week thinking I didn't care and good riddance, and then...and then, one morning...I saw a glowworm, making its way up the stairs, step by step the worm climbed, and yessir it took three whole days but I watched, *every single minute of it*, why it was climbing up the stairs, I don't know, *(Shrugging)* glowworms, and yet...watching it, I had a revelation that cracked my head right in two. I'm gonna win her back, Marveaux, and I'm gonna live like that worm,

striving, straining, climbing ever higher, and that,
that is why I'm off to the lake!

MARVEAUX: You cheated on her!? How dare you!
If she's at the lake, then that's where I'm going!
I'm going to win her love once and for all!

HALLIWELL: Wait a minute, Jack, weren't you listening?
That's where *I'm* going!

MARVEAUX: You had your chance, move aside.

HALLIWELL: Look, I mean it—

MARVEAUX: Lift up!

(*The doors to the lift close. We watch the indicator chart
the elevator's progress. A bell rings, the doors open, and*
HALLIWELL *and* MARVEAUX *collapse out of the elevator,
bloodied, clothes torn, both near death. They begin a painful
and painfully slow crawl on stomachs and sides to the lake,
holding each other back and administering intermittent kicks
to the groin.* MACMANN *appears from another part of stage
and crawls as well.*)

GOAT: Crawling towards the lake, the two of them
are...and look, there's Macmann, blind as a worm,
he's crawling toward the lake too.... Oh they're in pain,
make no mistake... (*Near tears and unbearable desperation*)
...but...but at least they know the cause of it! ...Even if
they're not the authors of it! There must be solace in
that!

MACMANN: Tree roots where I need them, to propel
myself forward....

HALLIWELL: It feels good to get the hands dirty again,
fingers in the soil...

MARVEAUX: A man needs to feel the earth every now
and then or he shall go mad....

(*Lights up on* TAXIDERMIST)

TAXIDERMIST: Now then, where were we little goat, yes
it's me, taxidermist, remember? I was attending to you
when that nice dying man arrived, and now that he left,
I'll answer any question you might have. (*Manipulating*
GOAT's *jaw—*)
"Oh goodie. You mentioned preservation chemicals.
What sir is their purpose?"
Well, the short answer is this—Lice and maggots.
They'll lay an egg in an untreated pelt and soon there's
a lousy and maggoty million infesting your corpus and
breeding and just imagine being the unwilling host to
those fellows wriggling and running rife through your
skin, uncaring, and unceasing, the wurbling, scattering,
scurrying, torturing creatures they are. A living hell
t'would be. A pain so horrible I bet you ten to one
it could bring you all the way back from the dead.
"And tell me this—do the chemicals always work?"
For a while. Not forever, no. No, all creatures bright
and beautiful, all creatures great and small, they all end
in maggots and in lice. But fear not, my little carcass of
a friend....you'll be in the incinerator long before then.
"But what if I'm not incinerated, what then? If I'm
preserved long enough to be infested, and no one
notices, what then?"
What then?
"Would I return to a sort of life?...and be forced to
concoct scenes of great beauty to distract from my
pain?"
You might at that.
"And what then?"
Well...you might concoct a scene even like this one.
Even with me. Putting on a gramophone record like
this...and Stroking your hide like this...and kissing your
head...on the occiput...the pointy bit...like this...and
telling you not to worry...not to worry...your end will
come...and you are loved....

(And as the gramophone music continues to play,
MACMANN *reaches the edge of the lake by a clump of bushes)*

MACMANN: It can't be denied...it's a body of water....
But how can I know that it's indeed the lake of my
youth? Blind as I am, for all I know this is merely a
rank puddle outside a slaughterhouse...

*(*MACMANN *concentrates...And we hear surging a rustle of
leaves, and birdsong, and the mysterious musical theme of the
lake we heard in* ACT ONE, *and* MACMANN *nods his head)*

MACMANN: No Macmann, tis the lake alright..you've
done it....Now off with shoes and socks, your moment
is near...but sssh..what is that I hear...

(We see HALLIWELL *at the lake, with* MARVEAUX *just
behind him.* PHILOMEL *appears as she did at the beginning
of the play, wearing a tail and reading a book on a rock in the
middle of the lake)*

MARVEAUX: Philomel! Don't listen to him—

HALLIWELL: I'm asking for another chance—
I've learned something invaluable—

MARVEAUX: Let me swim out to you, I can do it—
I know now something I didn't before—

PHILOMEL: *(Still clearly hurt by* HALLIWELL's *betrayal)*
So you've learned something, have you? Well then,
I will give you a chance to prove yourself. I fished
Halliwell's revolver out of the lake. It's lying on that
stump. I shall count to three. Whoever grabs the gun,
shoots the other and swims to me will have my love.

MARVEAUX: So this it...I shall miss you, Halliwell.

HALLIWELL: And I, you, Marveaux. I know that you
love her.

MARVEAUX: Though I don't know why.

HALLIWELL: That's not important. To swim toward love—that's all we can do.

MARVEAUX: Yes.

(They embrace tearfully, kissing each other's cheeks, and then—)

PHILOMEL: Are you ready? Here we go. One... Two...

(But before she reaches "three", MARVEAUX rushes toward the gun. Points it at HALLIWELL, then points it at his own head)

HALLIWELL: What are you doing?!

MARVEAUX: She loves you more. I'm ensuring your happiness.

HALLIWELL: You fool! Give me that gun—I was going to shoot myself first, but you cheated—

MARVEAUX: I love you, and I'm no longer afraid to die, so long as I die for love—my love for you, and her love for you, and your love for her.

HALLIWELL: But what about my love for *you*?

MARVEAUX: You'll get over it.

HALLIWELL: Like hell I will!

(HALLIWELL rushes MARVEAUX, trying to wrest the gun away.)

MARVEAUX: No! Let go! Philomel, make him stop— you love him more!

PHILOMEL: I hate you both, but I hate you a little less, Marveaux. *(Sincerely)* In fact, I think I could learn to love your simple heart.

HALLIWELL: There, do you hear that! Now give me that gun!

(HALLIWELL *wrests the gun away, brings it to head, but*
MARVEAUX *rushes in, grabs gun. They are wrestling on*
ground with gun, when we hear a shot accidentally fired
while MARVEAUX *is on top. Pause.* HALLIWELL *slowly*
rolls MARVEAUX *over, who lies dead.)*

HALLIWELL: What have I done? ...All right then...
if this is how it has to be...

(HALLIWELL *plunges into the water and begins swimming,*
churning arms and legs)

PHILOMEL: Then you're coming after all.

HALLIWELL: I certainly am.

PHILOMEL: But you don't even know if I love you
anymore.

HALLIWELL: No I don't.

PHILOMEL: Or if you'll make it.

HALLIWELL: I know only this....
(He is pulled under the waves and comes up again.)
That a man...can only be judged by what he attempts,
not by what he accomplishes....

(He is pulled under the waves and comes up again.)

PHILOMEL: But will you reach me or not?

HALLIWELL: It doesn't even matter. For all I can do is all
I can do, and all I, or any man, can do, is swim toward
love....
(He is pulled under the waves, then struggles to the surface.)
I know that you're bitter—
(He is pulled under the waves, then struggles to the surface.)
—But with perseverance, we can work through it—

PHILOMEL: If you only knew how much you hurt me—

HALLIWELL: I know...I know....
(He is pulled under, then struggles up again.)
I don't know if I can do it!

(He goes under, and struggles up again.)
Philomel, I'm going to need your help!
(He goes under and struggles up again.)
If you have any love for me left—

*(HALLIWELL goes under and struggles up again, arms and
legs churning, swimming toward PHILOMEL with everything
that's in him)*

HALLIWELL: I will make it, I—

*(HALLIWELL goes under and struggles up again. Goes under
and struggles up again, spluttering and gasping each time.
PHILOMEL stays impassive, or tries to concentrate on her
book as HALLIWELL disappears and comes up three more
times. He treads water successfully for a few seconds,
swimming toward her—)*

HALLIWELL: Philomel, I love—
(He goes under again and comes up.)
Damn it, I love—

*(He goes under again and comes up. He repeats this three
times, with each time it seeming like his last, then, a pause
above the waves, and he sinks. PHILOMEL, who had been
struggling with herself all the while, then calls out—)*

PHILOMEL: Halliwell! Don't give up! Halliwell!
I love you! I love you! Don't...don't...die...oh what
have I done...what have I done....

*(She cries softly as we hear a pathetic singing in the distance,
getting nearer, and now the ELDER HALLIWELL appears,
beyond exhausted)*

ELDER HALLIWELL: *(Sings)*
When the corn is waving la la dear...
To hear thy la la voice la
...winning smile...
The moon...
The stars will brightly...
(He stops when he sees—) The lake! Look! The lake! Man

alive that was a long walk. Well I made it. Now then, what was it I came here for.... *(Pause)* Mind's a blank.... *(Pause)* ...Bananas? ...No...but it was something like bananas...I can't remember what bananas are now... wait, they're furniture, and furniture are things you wear, wait, I've got it, pants, that's what bananas are, they're pants! That's what I was looking for, the trousers of my youth, and there they are! *(He goes over to a pair of trousers lying by the bank or hanging on a branch. He tries them on but they seem quite small. He sits on ground and tries to put them on, rolls about in his struggle, then finally realizes—)* These aren't my trousers. And what's this on the ground, is it a bicycle...no...no, it's a corpse.... *(He gradually becomes more lucid, shaking off his senility.)* ...and I think I know him...yes...that's Marveaux, my son's childhood friend.... My god, what's happened....

PHILOMEL: He's dead...

ELDER HALLIWELL: He had a friend...his name was Halliwell...Do you happen to know what happened to him?

(PHILOMEL can say nothing, but bursts into tears)

ELDER HALLIWELL: Well that I should live to see it.... A siren who has become a victim of Love herself....

PHILOMEL: I can't bear it....

ELDER HALLIWELL: For a son to die before his father... it's a blow you can't recover from.

PHILOMEL: My heart's in a hundred pieces.

ELDER HALLIWELL: I'm tired.

PHILOMEL: Then come with me. Beneath the waves—

ELDER HALLIWELL: Yes O Philomel. Beneath the crags—

PHILOMEL: —the crashes and clamours—

ELDER HALLIWELL: —the thunderings—

PHILOMEL: —the claspings and asunderings that
never cease—

ELDER HALLIWELL: —but beneath the waves,
O Philomel, we'll sit, and not stir.

PHILOMEL: Where all is silent as fishes...

ELDER HALLIWELL: ...as silent as a sea-green grave....

(ELDER HALLIWELL *plunges into the water and drowns
and* PHILOMEL *disappears beneath the waves as well.
Now* MARVEAUX *revives with a groan as* MACMANN
resumes his crawl to the lake.)

MARVEAUX: (*As he slowly crawls to lake*) What a pointless
earth this is...the only answer is to drag myself to the
lake and drown.

MACMANN: I'm on my way there too. Am I headed in
the general direction?

MARVEAUX: Straight on and you'll be fine. You can
follow me if you like.

MACMANN: I'm much obliged.

MARVEAUX: I hope it isn't too difficult to drown.

MACMANN: I think it's stones we're needing. For the
pockets.

MARVEAUX: Of course! To weigh us down! I'd never
have thought of that.

MACMANN: (*Picking up a stone*) I think this is a good one.

MARVEAUX: That's a wonderful rock. (*Finding a stone*)
Here, feel this.

MACMANN: Oh this is the best rock yet.

MARVEAUX: Here, take it.

MACMANN: What? I couldn't.

MARVEAUX: I mean it. Please.

MACMANN: (*Awfully moved, but—*) No, no I can't....
The world isn't kind, ideals are fables, and as I crawl
to my death, I don't want anything to try to convince
me otherwise....

MARVEAUX: Yes, and yet—

MACMANN: —ssh.....do you hear something?

(*Now softly, a shimmering, mysterious sort of music.
And now softly, but getting louder, the sound of galloping
hooves. They become abnormally loud, accompanied by an
otherworldly whinnying.*)

MARVEAUX: It's...impossible....

MACMANN: What is it?

MARVEAUX: It is written that it approaches the bank of
a lake each evening as the sun is setting, and yet, who'd
have thought—

MACMANN: What is it.

(*Lights up on the actor playing the* GOAT, *with a horn affixed
to the middle of his forehead. He, perhaps, is wearing a clean,
white union suit for the occasion.*)

MARVEAUX: (*Agape with awe and wonder*)...a creature
personifying nobility and purity, and dignity and
innocence and sincerity, wisdom and strength, and
vulnerability. In short....Supreme Beauty. It is a shame
you are blind.

MACMANN: At this moment...I am not blind... Let us
listen to the divine wisdom that will issue from his
mouth...

UNICORN: This walk to the lake gets longer every day,
to wash, to lake to wash, but it's important to wash and
soap is very important in the matter of washing and I
stand by Swan's. Swan's Soap. Swaaan's. It's the lather

you see, it's very nice, but best of all, it floats. The soap.
There, see that! There it is, floating. It's nice to see
floating soap. How they do it is a mystery. A miracle.
They say it's because it's so pure you see. What's pure?
Maggotless and liceless? Well, that's a good start, but
purity is more than that. Cut it open. You'll see. There's
no bitterness or gloom in the making of it, so you won't
find it in the soap. And you won't find any unniceness,
or cynicism or spite, or despair in the soap. No.
Just soap. But I don't begin to understand it and
it's a mystery to me. But its purity washes all the dirt
away, so I use it when I can.... Alright, I'm off now.

(We hear the thundering of hooves fading into the distance.)

MARVEAUX: He's gone....

MACMANN: Shall we continue on, then?

MARVEAUX: Strange....the lake has never looked as...
as flat as it does now.

MACMANN: Poets say "placid" or "unpeturbéd by
vexsome gusts." You might want to try one of those.

MARVEAUX: I know what poets say. But I'm telling you,
what it really looks is "flat." There used to be highs
and lows due to the whirlpools and swirling eddies,
but now the lake looks like it's gone to the place it was
always yearning for...nothing scenic, nothing poetic...
no...just...flat...flat and level.

MACMANN: Wait a minute. Say that again.

MARVEAUX: ...Flat...and level.

MACMANN: *(Eyes shining)* That's it.... That's it! That's it!

MARVEAUX: What?

MACMANN: Water always finds its own level.

MARVEAUX: It does?

MACMANN: Yes, it's a scientific principle—

MARVEAUX: *(Tears in eyes)* It's beautiful...

MACMANN: *(Huge tears in eyes, ecstatic)* It is...so... beautiful....

MARVEAUX: Water always finds its own level.... Is it true? Does it always?

MACMANN: Always, my friend. There might be struggle and strife but it does. And it's a principle that everybody's taught, but no one has done what seems so obvious now *can* be done!

MARVEAUX: What are you talking about?

MACMANN: A ballcock! A rod connected to a ballcock... a cistern that fills with water until it *finds its own level* and triggers the mechanism to *shut itself off*!

MARVEAUX: You mean—

MACMANN: Yes! Based on the irrefutable principle that water always finds it's own level, I will create a symphonic discharge system allowing a toilet to flush effectively when the cistern is only half full! And you will help me—

MARVEAUX: Oh no, not I, I don't know the first thing about—

MACMANN: But I do! And with your vision and my know-how, what can't we accomplish?! Say you will... Oh say you will....

(Pause, then grin steals across MARVEAUX's *face.)*

MARVEAUX: ...Yes...yes...I will ...

(They embrace, as music swells to a great and soaring climax.)

GOAT: And that's the story I set out to tell from the very beginning. The story of how the Silent Valveless Water Waste Preventer, British Patent 4990, was invented. The end. The end. For them at least....I....I am....still

here....Bah. *(Bleating realistically—)* Baaaah...
(Considers—) Water always finds its own level....
(Sincerest of confessions—) I have something to say.
I am not a tramcar conductor. No. Nor an ailing
mother. No. Or thoroughbred. Or taxidermist.
Or heroic dog. Or father and channel swimmer.
Or passimeter booking equipment supervisor.
And I'm certainly not..a unicorn. No. I am a goat.
I know. I'm saying it. I am a goat. You see. We all find
our own level. In the end. Bah. And yet, everything
endures, despite of it, doesn't it. Or rather, *because* of it.
Yes...we can stay just where we are, at our very own
level....and endure...
(Resigned to it—)
I'll endure....
(Now perhaps seeing a positive—if not a beautiful—
side to it—)
I will. I will...I will.... Endure....

(Utterly beautiful music swells as it is revealed that
the GOAT *is part of a remarkably lovely crèche scene.*
Then lights out, and up on music—perhaps **Paper Moon**
as sung by Cliff Edwards)

END OF PLAY